THE IRON INDIANS

by

Rene A. Henry

Based on the 1953 William & Mary Football Team

Gollywobbler Productions

LIBRARY OF CONGRESS CATALOGING-IN-PUBLICATION DATA

Henry, Rene A. (1933-   )
    The Iron Indians
    Rene A. Henry – 1st ed.
        p.   cm.
    Includes biographical references and index
    ISBN# 978-0-9674535-3-8
    1. The College of William and Mary. 2. Football. 3. Sports.
    4. Iron Indians. 5. History. 6. 1953. 7. Fabulous Fifties.
    8. Williamsburg, Virginia. I. Title

Library of Congress Control Number: 2001012345

© 2011, Rene A. Henry
Gollywobbler Productions
Seattle, Washington

All rights reserved. No part of this book may be reproduced or transmitted in any form or by any means, electrical or mechanical, including photocopying, recording, or by any information storage and retrieval system without permission in writing from the copyright owner.

First Edition, 2011

10 9 8 7 6 5 4 3 2 1

Printed in the United States of America

The screenplay for a feature motion picture, *The Iron Indians* is registered with the Writers Guild of America, West, Inc., No. 1447440

For information contact:
Rene A. Henry
1474 21st Avenue
Seattle, Washington 98122
Phone – 206-329-4422
Email: rene@renehenry.com

Special Thanks

This project would not have been possible without the help of family and friends of the 24 Iron Indians and many other people, some of whom made significant contributions. The author wishes to thank the following:

Joseph ('53) and Eloise Bryant Agee ('53); Archives of *The Flat Hat*; Archives of the Earl Gregg Swem Library; John "Jeep" Bednarik (54); William A. ('54) and Barbara Crosset ('54) Brink; Joseph M. Cardaci ('54); Barbara Ann Pharo Henley Cheshire ('56); Pete Clawson, W&M Sports Information Director; Charles Copeland ('55); Dr. Karen R. Cottrell ('66, M.Ed.'69, Ed.D. '84); Frank H. "Sonny" Cowling, Sr. ('53); Earl Linwood ('55) and Shelly Jane Bailey ('55) Cox; Alexandra Bettiger "Sandy" Crenier ('54); Jennings Culley, Richmond, Virginia.; Jim Ducibella, W&M University Relations; Bette Bodley Dunker ('54); Aubrey ('56) and Susan Richardson Fitzgerald ('57); Jane Achenbach Freeman ('47); Tom Garrett, Suffolk, Virginia; Denys Grant ('58); Ann Callihan Hines Greene ('54); Nicholas A. Grieco, Essex Fells, N.J.; J. Edward Grimsley ('51, LLD '11); Lisa M. Guthrie, Richmond, Virginia.; C. Gerald ('53) and Ann Johnson Harris ('53); Doug Henley, Jr., Durham, N.C.; Patricia Lee Rustad Herrmann ('55); Ross Hindmarsh ('58); J. Edward "Bud" Jay ('54); Peter M. Kalison ('57); Louis Lambert Kale, W&M The Historic Campus; Elaine Elias Kappel ('55); James S. Kelly ('51); Leah D. Kelly, Monmouth Beach, N.J.; Ben Kennedy ('05); Alton S. ('53) and Joann Lore Kersey ('53); Otto Lowe Jr. ('55, BCL '58); Dr. James B. McNeer, President, Richard Bland College; Dr. John C. ('55) and Carol Butters ('54) Marsh; Joseph C. Mark ('50); Dr. William "Bill" Marfizo ('56); William "Bill" Martin ('55); The late Grover "Tommy" ('54) and Katherine ('51) Martin; Jeff Maurer, *The Daily American,* Somerset, Pennsylvania; Steve Milkovich ('54); Curt Miller, North East, Maryland; Martha Mills, University of North Carolina Alumni Relations; Doug Mosley, Sports Information Director, University of Cincinnati; Gerald Murchison ('55); *Newport News Daily Press; Norfolk Virginian Pilot;* Lawrence Peccatiello ('58); Eric Pesola, W&M Alumni Association; Donna M. Potts, W&M Alumni Association; W. Taylor Reveley III, President W&M; *Richmond Times-Dispatch*; John Risjord ('55); William "Bill" Riley (Class of '56), Frederick, Maryland; W. Samuel Sadler ('64, M.Ed. '71); Jerry ('55) and Dorothy Bailey ('53) Sazio; Amy Schindler, University Archivist, Earl Gregg Swem Library; Agnes Egger "Lollie" Scott ('55); Stacy Smith, Human Resources, Chesapeake (Virginia) Public Schools; Charles Sumner ('55) and June Raymond, Lahaina, Maui, Hawai'i; Barbara Thompson, Virginia Beach (Virginia) Schools; William F. "Bill" Tucker, Sr. ('58); Gordon ('54) and Dr. Elizabeth Lee Davis Vliet ('68, M.Ed. '71); Linda Waksmunski, Severna Park, Maryland; Edward A. ('56) and Belinda Beach Owens ('56) Watkins; Warren Weiss ('54); Patricia Woolfolk, Assistant to the President, Richard Bland College.

Table of Contents

The Iron Indians   1

    The Fabulous Fifties   1
    The Cost of Living   2
    Sports   3
    Television and Radio   3
    The Movies, Broadway, Music and Books   4
    On the W&M Campus   5
    Life On Campus   8
    A Football Season Or Not?   10
    Football Was Different In the 50s   12
    The First Day of Practice   12
    W&M 16 – Wake Forest 14   13
    W&M 6 – Navy 6   14
    Cincinnati 57 – W&M 7   15
    W&M 13 – Virginia Tech 7   15
    W&M 12 – George Washington 7   16
    W&M 7 – North Carolina State 6   16
    VMI 20 – W&M 19   16
    W&M 21 – Richmond 0   17
    Washington & Lee 33 – W&M 7   17
    Boston University 41 – W&M 14   17
    Campus Love   18
    Fun and Jokes   18
    Jerry Sazio and Dot Bailey   19
    Charlie Copeland and Charlene Foster   20
    Nicknames and Anecdotes   20
    A Very Tight Budget   22
    Excitement In the Burg – A Panty Raid   23
    The Season Finale   24

Roster of Players   26

The Schedule   26

The 24 Iron Indians   27

    John "Jeep" Bednarik   27
    Bill Bowman   28
    Charles Copeland   28
    Linwood Cox   29
    Robert E. "Bob" Elzey   30
    Aubrey Fitzgerald   30
    Al Grieco   31
    Doug Henley   31
    Walter "Shorty" Herrmann   32
    L. Quinby Hines   32
    George Karschner   33
    William "Bill" Marfizo   33

William "Bill" Martin	34
Grover T. "Tommy" Martin	34
Steve Milkovich	35
Bill Nagy	35
George Parozzo	36
Jack Place	36
Bill Riley	37
John Risjord	37
Jerry Sazio	38
Sam Scott	39
Charlie Sumner	39
Chet Waksmunski	40

The Coaches and Staff — **41**

John J. "Jack" Freeman	41
Eric Tipton	44
Herbert "Neepie" Miller	44
Boydson Baird	45
Joseph C. Mark	46
John L. Clements	46
Frank H. "Sonny" Cowling, Sr.	47
Guilford M. "Bill" Joyner	47
William S. "Pappy" Gooch	48
Rene A. Henry	48

The Season — **50**

Iron Indians Saves W&M by Jennings Culley	52
W&M v. Wake Forest	54
W&M v. Navy	59
W&M v. Cincinnati	63
W&M v. Virginia Tech	67
W&M v. George Washington	71
W&M v. North Carolina State	75
W&M v. VMI	79
W&M v. Richmond	83
W&M v. Washington & Lee	87
W&M v. Boston University	91

Sports Information

The sports information director is generally the most underpaid and in many instances under appreciated of all senior management in any college or university athletic department. This also is the only office in the athletic department that provides a service for every public and interested party – the athletes, coaches, students, parents, faculty, administration, fund raisers, fans, sportswriters and broadcasters, prospective student-athletes and professional recruiters.

Historically, the office has been responsible for preparing daily news releases, media guides, event programs and any publication related to the sports program as well as archiving information for future use. In today's world, the department is now communicating with thousands of people on a daily basis through the college's webpage, using video, audio and a wide variety of social networking platforms. Last year the site, http://www.tribeathletics.com, had more than 500,000 visitors.

If you value the ability to meaningfully stay in contact with Tribe sports, please support the department at William & Mary by making a tax-deductible contribution to the Rene A. Henry Sports Information Endowment and sending it to P.O. Box 399, Williamsburg, VA 23187.

The Iron Indians – The Movie

The story of the 1953 William & Mary Iron Indians is being developed into a feature motion picture by Rene A. Henry and Oscar-nominated producer Gabor Nagy. The screenplay is registered with the Writers Guild of America, West, Inc., No. 1447440.

Anyone, especially alumni and supporters of the College, interested in seeing this project brought to the screen and participating in the project should contact Mr. Henry at rene@renehenry.com.

The Iron Indians

The 1953 William & Mary "Iron Indians" football team was extraordinary. With only 24 players and only 15 scholarships, Jack Freeman accomplished what few coaches could do today. Many would not even attempt the challenge. The team lost only once in its first six games but as the season progressed, injuries eventually took their toll. The team finished with a 5-4-1 record. It wasn't until 1965 that W&M had another winning football season.

The players were remarkable young men. All were outstanding athletes. Many were campus leaders. Most excelled in the classroom. One was Phi Beta Kappa and elected to Omicron Delta Kappa. Several were Dean's List. Two were pre-season Academic all-Americans. Several grew up in small Pennsylvania coal mine towns. All went on to successful careers. Five were veterans returning from active military service in Korea or the South Pacific. Most went into one of the armed forces after graduation, some having their professional careers either interrupted or put on hold for two years.

Three became prominent attorneys. Six of the players were drafted by or signed professional contracts with National Football League teams. Two had outstanding careers in the NFL and one in the Canadian professional football league. Many married their college sweethearts in what became lifetime relationships. One was named "Mr. Formal" his senior year. One player married the homecoming queen and another married "Miss William & Mary." They all were outstanding individuals!

The Fabulous Fifties

As the decade of the Fabulous Fifties began, the United States had hardly recovered from World War II when our military resources were already in the third year of an escalating war in Korea. President Harry S. Truman had just fired General Douglas MacArthur as the supreme commander of the United Nations Command. In his farewell address to a joint session of Congress on April 19, 1951, MacArthur gave us a new soundbite: "Old soldiers never die, they just fade away."

The coronation of Queen Elizabeth II was held in Westminster Abbey on February 6, 1952, more than a year after she had ascended to the throne upon the death of her father, King George VI. After the Conservative Party lost in 1945, Winston Churchill won a narrow victory to become Britain's Prime Minister a second time. In her first political campaign, Margaret Thatcher, who would be chancellor of The College of William &

Mary from 1993-2000, became the youngest conservative candidate to be elected to Parliament. In Argentina, Juan Peron was re-elected president and his wife Eva Peron, famous for "Don't Cry For Me, Argentina," was the new vice president.

Senator Joseph McCarthy (R-Wisconsin) and his Committee on Un-American Activities targeted almost everyone as a Communist or member of a Communist front organization. Actor Charlie Chaplin, one of the many accused in Hollywood, left the U.S. to live in Britain and FBI Director J. Edgar Hoover revoked his right to ever return. Julius and Ethel Rosenberg were condemned to death in the electric chair for passing nuclear secrets to the Soviets. They were executed at Sing Sing prison in Ossining, New York.

The 22nd Amendment to the U.S. Constitution was passed limiting presidents to two terms. The West Germans invented 33 rpm long play vinyl records which would compete with the smaller 45 rpm discs. Chevrolet introduced the Corvette. New York adopted three color traffic lights – red, yellow and green. Research reported that cigarette smoking causes lung cancer. Sir Edmund Hillary and his Sherpa, Tenzing Norgay, became the first climbers to reach the summit of Mt. Everest in Nepal.

Dr. Jonas Salk discovered the polio vaccine. Joseph Stalin died after nearly a quarter of a century of being Russia's undisputed leader. In Cuba, Fidel Castro launched the "26th of July Movement" rebellion against the Batista regime. With the help of the CIA, Mohammad Rezā Shāh Pahlavi, the Shah of Iran was restored to power. Albert Schweitzer and General George C. Marshall were awarded the Nobel Peace Prize.

The Cost of Living

The average cost of a gallon of gasoline was only 20 cents. The average cost of a new car was $1,650 and Fords ranged in price from $1,537 to $2,403. Studebaker introduced dramatic new styling created by designer Raymond Loewy. Automobile manufacturers stimulated a buy now-pay later mentality and allowed buyers longer periods of time to pay for a car. The average worker earned $4,011 a year. The average cost of a new house was $17,400. Bread was 16 cents a loaf, milk 94 cents a gallon, romaine lettuce 10 cents a pound, a 10-pound bag of C&H sugar cost 89 cents, a 16-ounce jar of Kraft Cheese Whiz 57 cents and a 12-ounce jar of Libby's pickles 25 cents.

It cost only 3 cents to mail a first class letter, we had a one penny postcard, and the postal service delivered mail to many homes and offices twice a day. People paid in cash for purchases and collected S&H Green Stamps to redeem for merchandise. Credit cards were limited to gasoline companies and retailers. Personal debt was minimal. There were no ATM machines. Diners Club introduced the first independent credit card in the world in 1950 but it would be another 15 years before we saw the proliferation we know today of bank and other travel and entertainment charge cards.

There were no giant discount stories like Costco, Wal-Mart, Target or K-Mart. But you could order almost anything you wanted – even a house – from the Sears, Roebuck catalog.

Sports

The New York Yankees beat the Brooklyn Dodgers in six games to win their fifth straight World Series. Ted Williams, one of baseball's greatest hitters, rejoined the Boston Red Sox after being recalled as a Marine Corps fighter pilot in Korea. Williams turned down offers to play baseball for service teams and instead flew 39 combat missions. On February 16 his plane was hit by enemy fire knocking out his hydraulics and electrical system, but he flew his damaged Panther Jet to an Air Force Base, escaped uninjured and was awarded the Air Medal. Rocky Marciano knocked out Jersey Joe Walcott in the first round to win the world heavyweight boxing championship. Bevo Francis, 6'9" basketball center at Rio Grande College in Ohio, scored 116 points against Ashland (Kentucky) Junior College and went on to average more than 50 points a game for the entire season.

Television and Radio

Television was in its infancy. There was no live television west of Pittsburgh. Television stations in the rest of the country broadcast programs a day later using kinescopes made by the networks by having a motion picture camera in front of a small television set. Drama programs like *Playhouse 90* were performed live by the actors.

People who had small black-and-white sets were watching Sid Caesar and Imogene Coca on *Your Show of Shows*, Red Skelton, Bob Hope, Milton Berle, Jackie Gleason, Red Buttons, Perry Como, Liberace, Danny Thomas in *Make Room for Daddy, Adventures of Ozzie and Harriett, Our Miss Brooks, George Burns and Gracie Allen,* boxing sponsored by Gillette on Wednesday nights, *What's My Line,* NBC's 15-minute nightly *Camel News Caravan* evening news with John Cameron Swayze, and *Your Hit Parade* with Dorothy Collins and Snooky Lanson singing the popular songs of the day.

"Guiding Light" had just premiered and became the longest running entertainment program in television history. In November, Edward R. Murrow debuted his *Person to Person* interview program. Dave Garroway hosted NBC's popular morning *The Today Show* with his sidekick, J. Fred Muggs, a chimpanzee. Arthur Godfrey was on both CBS radio and television with his 90-minute, mid-morning program. Steve Allen filled in for Godfrey one evening on *Talent Scouts* and became an overnight celebrity. A year later Allen was the first host of NBC's *Tonight Show.* Children watched *Howdy Doody* and *Kukla, Fran and Ollie.* The first issue of *TV Guide* was published for 10 cities.

In January, Truman became the first U.S. president to broadcast his farewell address on both radio and television. President Dwight D. Eisenhower, who continued the tradition, was given an honorary degree at William & Mary in the Spring of 1953 at the inauguration of Admiral Alvin Duke Chandler as the college's 22nd president. Hollywood was worried that people would stay home and watch television rather than go to the movie theater, so the wide-screen process was developed. *The Robe* was the first movie produced in Cinemascope.

Radio was very popular and some of our favorite shows included Bing Crosby, Dean Martin and Jerry Lewis, Edgar Bergen and Charlie McCarthy, *Perry Mason, Fibber McGee and Molly, Green Hornet, Gunsmoke, Amos 'n' Andy, Dragnet, Lone Ranger, Abbott and Costello, Lum and Abner, The Great Gildersleeve*, an abundance of 15-minute soap operas, and news reports by H.V. Kaltenborn. On Saturday morning opera lovers could always listen to the Metropolitan from New York City. Texas Instruments introduced the first transistor radio.

The Movies, Broadway, Music and Books

The movies we went to see in the theater included *Singin' In the Rain, Lili, Gentlemen Prefer Blondes, By the Light of the Silvery Moon, Shane*, and *From Here to Eternity*. The Academy of Motion Picture Arts & Sciences awarded the Oscar for best film to Cecil B. DeMille's *The Greatest Show On Earth*. Gary Cooper in *High Noon* and Shirley Booth in *Come Back Little Sheba* won for best actor and Anthony Quinn in *Viva Zapata* and Gloria Grahame in *The Bad and the Beautiful* won for the best supporting roles.

On Broadway *Wonderful Town* won the TONY for best musical and Arthur Miller's *The Crucible* won for best play. Other shows playing then included The Solid Gold Cadillac, Picnic, Can-Can, Porgy and Bess, Tea and Sympathy, and Kismet, which would win a TONY in 1954.

The Pulitzer Prize for fiction went to Ernest Hemingway for *The Old Man and the Sea*. Ian Fleming published his first James Bond novel, *Casino Royale*. Hugh Hefner published the first issue of *Playboy* with Marilyn Monroe nude on the cover. The best-selling fiction books were *The Robe, The Silver Chalice, Battle Cry, From Here to Eternity* and *The High and the Mighty*. All were made into popular motion pictures. The Holy Bible continued to lead nonfiction sales. Other popular books were Norman Vincent Peale's *The Power of Positive Thinking*, Alfred Kinsey's *Sexual Behavior in the Human Female* and *A Man Called Peter* by Catherine Marshall.

The music we listened to reflected on the post-World War II optimism in our country and became the feel-good innocence of the Decade of the Fifties. Tops on *Your Hit Parade* were *I Saw Mommy Kissing Santa Claus*; Perry Como's *Don't Let the Stars Get in Your Eyes*; Les Paul and Mary Ford performing *Vaya Con Dios*; Patti Page singing *The Doggie in the Window*; Hank Williams' *Your Cheatin' Heart*; Dean Martin's *That's Amore*; The Ames Brothers' *You, You, You*; and Teresa Brewer singing *Till I Waltz Again With You*. The Big Band Era or Swing Era that originated in the 1930s and the music of Benny Goodman, Tommy Dorsey and Glenn Miller continued to be a driving force in music. Teenagers liked the new sound of Rock and Roll which took off in 1955 when Bill Haley recorded "Rock Around the Clock."

We had an abundance of magazines and newspapers. There were great articles *in Life, Look, Collier's, Time* and *The Saturday Evening Post*. Characters on the comics page included *Dick Tracy, Blondie, Terry and the Pirates, Henry, Little Orphan Annie, Archie* and *Our Boarding House With Major Hoople*.

On the W&M Campus

Meanwhile, in Williamsburg, Virginia, the faculty, administration and 1,500 students at The College of William & Mary had hardly ended celebrating the 1953 New Year when a crisis in mid-January sent shock waves through the campus.

Students had removed the hinges of a door in Blow Gymnasium that led to the Military Science Department and stole an ROTC final exam. They shared the exam with others who were taking the class. Many were athletes. Those involved had obviously forgotten or completely disregarded the time during orientation week when freshmen were brought into a dark room, met by black robed upperclassmen, and the only light was from a single candle to impress upon everyone the significance of the W&M Honor Code. In 1779, when then Governor Thomas Jefferson, who graduated in 1762, reorganized the college, W&M became the first college in the country to have an Honor System. Every student took an oath pledging not to lie, cheat, steal or tolerate anyone who does.

Some 36 students were brought before the student-administered Honor Council. Those who had stolen or cheated on the exam or lied, were expelled. Some students who did not take the ROTC class, but knew that their roommate or a close friend was involved and did not report the violation, were suspended for "tolerating" the breach of the code. Sometime between the mid-1960s and 1970s the Honor Code was amended and the fourth point of "toleration" was excluded.

The Army colonel who prepared the exam deliberately made one question so difficult that he did not expect anyone to get a correct answer. With so many cheating and getting the correct answer, it immediately raised a red flag. Many of those were athletes. Joe D. Farrar, dean of men, called every athlete into his office and accused each of either cheating or stealing the exam or knowing who did. Magnetic tape recorders were new at the time. Farrar purchased one so he could record the conversations. When all was done, only a score of the football players would be returning to campus in the Fall. Eight starters and the two co-captains no longer were part of the W&M family.

The following letter was published on page one of the student newspaper, *The Flat Hat,* on February 17, 1953:

Letter From President To W&M Student Body

> The Honor Code was established at the College of William and Mary on the basis of individual responsibility. Since its establishment the Honor System has undergone severe tests. Its value, however, has been realized by many schools and colleges in our country and it students and the Honor Council which administers the Honor Code have risen to its support, and it has worked successfully at William and Mary over the years.
>
> As a result of the fact that the public press decided to publish certain matters affecting our Honor Code, it was necessary that the College make the following statement:
>
> "Infractions of the Honor Code involving certain students in the Department of Military Science and Tactics have been uncovered. Investigations are being made and appropriate

corrective measures have been and are being taken. It is not the policy of the College to release details regarding students involved in disciplinary matters."

The matters involved due to their very nature are the private affairs of the individuals concerned, and it is not the intention of our College to make any other statements.

The William and Mary student body is made up of the finest young men and women in our country. They have a deep regard for the sensibilities of others and the high character of the Honor Code.

A. D. Chandler

In the same edition of *The Flat Hat*, Arnold H. Lubasch, editor, wrote the following editorial:

The Honorable Thing

We were greatly shocked and chagrined by the disclosure of prolific violations of the Honor System which came to light during the past week. It seems particularly regrettable that William and Mary, proud originator of the Honor System for American colleges in 1779, should fall victim to such flagrant violations of the Honor Code.

It is a known fact that extensive Honor System violations occurred in the College's department of Military Science and Tactics. We can neither deny nor ignore the seriousness and scope of the present situation. The College has stated that "appropriate and corrective measures" have been taken to punish the guilty parties and to preserve the Honor System at William and Mary.

The names and number of the individuals involved, the circumstances under which the violations occurred, and the various details of the entire unsavory affair are of relatively minor significance here. We are in complete agreement with President Chandler and the College that "the matters involved due to their very nature, are the private affairs of the individuals concerned."

We believe that dirty linen should be washed in public where everyone can see that it has been thoroughly cleaned and no longer is dirty. Honor System violations occurred; the guilty parties are being punished; the Honor System, as we know it, is being preserved – these are facts that all the students of this College are entitled to know.

We believe that the personal aspects of the Honor System infractions should be kept confidential, although we feel it would be advantageous to release the more general details of the affair in order to pacify the press and stop vicious rumors which continue to circulate. But these are not the vital issues that demand our scrutiny at this time. The real issue at stake is honor itself.

We believe that honor, by very definition, is a personal thing and cannot be regulated or enforced by others. We cannot be held responsible for the honor of others nor can others be held responsible for our honor. To remove honor from a personal basis is to destroy it. We are not convinced that people can be compelled to report the Honor System violations of others or that an ethical principle exists to force them to do so.

This does not mean that students should not report Honor System violations – it means that they should not be compelled to do so. This is a question of personal ethics and honor which each individual must answer for himself. Under the present circumstances, however, we must all realistically recognize that we have signed a particular Honor code.

There can be no compromise with honor if we are to preserve it. Personal honor and integrity remain our most cherished possessions. Those who cheat and violate their personal honor lose their most valuable possession – self-respect. The dishonorable individual must inevitably pay the price of his dishonor. The basic foundation of the Honor System is a personal responsibility and integrity upon the part of the individuals involved. It is a question of personal ethics that each individual must face for himself.

We do not believe that anyone who has ever operated under a real Honor System would ever be content under any other system. For us, any other system would be unbearable.

The disclosure of Honor System violations was a grave blow to the College, but it was not the first blow sustained by this College, although we sincerely hope that it will be the last. William and Mary has suffered and survived many such crises in the past and it will certainly survive this one. As in the past, we hope that the College will emerge strengthened as a result of its present difficulties.

The "late unpleasantness" has a persistent habit of lingering on. It is the solemn responsibility of every one of us to help the College overcome its present difficulties and continue with increased vigor– it is the honorable thing to do.

A.H.L.

The crisis happened in the middle of the basketball season and the W&M basketball team also was decimated by the crisis. When W&M beat a favored Duke 85-82 on February 19 in Blow Gym with only six players, sportswriters asked what happened to the other players. The scandal became public. The college was non-responsive and refused to discuss the issue. The media then gathered whatever information it could from any available source, most completely uninformed, and speculated with articles and columns.

This so angered Lubasch that he wrote a subsequent editorial on February 24, 1953:

Journalistic Policies

The current Honor System controversy at William and Mary has received considerable editorial comment in the State newspapers. Under the present circumstances, these newspapers certainly have the right, and perhaps even the duty, to discuss the College's Honor System on their editorial pages. We believe, however, that much of this editorial comment in the public press has been made without the benefit of factual information and sufficient understanding. The unfortunate result could only be a fallacious misrepresentation of the situation.

In addition to the distorted editorials which appeared locally, an abundance of perfidious news coverage entered newspapers throughout the country. With a most regrettable display of yellow journalism, many of these papers transformed the problem into a spurious athletic scandal with vicious and false connotations. Much of the unfavorable publicity might have been avoided had an adequate news report been forthcoming from the College, but this in no way excuses the yellow journalism that ensued.

Far be it for the *Flat Hat* to attack freedom of the press or question the irrevocable right of the daily papers to exercise it, but we believe it is essential that these newspapers always remember their responsibilities as well as their rights. In the present instance, we do not believe the newspapers as a whole were true to their obligation to report the news with accuracy and to interpret it with justice.

Newspapers are often subjected to undue pressure to exploit the sensational aspects of the news and to present editorial comment which conforms to particular vested opinions. The ability to overcome the pressure is one of the major factors that distinguishes a good newspaper from a poor one.

As for the *Flat Hat*, this newspaper will stand by the policy stated in the opening editorial of the semester, "We will strive for complete and accurate coverage of all pertinent news in the College community" and comment editorially "with complete honesty, careful thought and sincere conviction."

We will not be intimidated or unduly influenced by those who believe the *Flat Hat* should avoid all controversial issues or those who believe the *Flat Hat* should offer sensational and destructive criticism. Whether the subject be the Honor System or keeping off the grass, the opinions expressed in this column will be our own. No censorship is exercised over the *Flat Hat* other than the discretion and integrity of the editors.

A.H.L.

For several weeks, the newspaper was deluged with letters from students and faculty, pro and con on the fourth point of the Honor Code. Some questioned the interpretation of honor as being different today than 175 years ago. One wrote that honor cannot be enforced. Others compared it to an ethical obligation. There was discussion about honor, ethics and loyalty. Some believed that the Honor Code needed to be modernized.

Before the end of April, a student committee chaired by future governor John Dalton proposed a detailed and written Honor Code Procedure. It was the most detailed and comprehensive summary of the Code in its history.

Life On Campus

In the Fifties there was no such thing as social media. Tweets were the sounds of birds in the Spring by Lake Matoaka or in the Sunken Gardens. A blackberry was something you ate. Greeks were a very important part of social life and most of the students were members of fraternities or sororities. Women were not permitted to have dates or to be with a man after 7 p.m. on Mondays. With the exception of Saturdays, when most of the social activity centered on the 11 fraternity lodges, women had to be inside their dormitories or sorority houses by 10 p.m. Those coeds who were on the Dean's List had the privilege of being able to stay out until 11 p.m. during weekdays. Dating a really smart coed had its advantages. Midnight was the final hour on Saturday.

In the late afternoons in the Spring and Fall the men loved to hang out around College Corner where Richmond and Jamestown Roads intersected with the Duke of Gloucester Street and North and South Boundary Streets. It was more commonly called Jockey

Corner. Some of the male students would sit on the steps of the Methodist Church or on a bench near the entrance to Wren Yard. Another popular spot was a bench on Jamestown Road near the Morris House where some of the athletes lived. Some athletes would sit on this bench even if they lived in another dormitory. The coeds walking from their dormitories to the cafeteria or post office would pass by these male "hang outs." These were the places the male students checked out the coeds. For some W&M students this was their first meeting place. Many blossomed into romances.

After dinner in the college cafeteria or at Danny's Campus Grill or a snack in the Wigwam, or on their way back from the post office, students would generally pass by Jockey Corner. Depending on individual budgets and available spending money, some might stop by Howard Johnson's for an ice cream cone and get the latest news and gossip from Jim Seu. The Wigwam was the closest thing in those days to a McDonald's today. Coffee was coffee – not a double caffé mocha or decaf expresso macchiato.

When someone wanted to splurge it might be a meal, snack or beer at the Corner Greeks, or even Chownings or Nick's in Yorktown. For a real dining experience it would be the King's Arms Tavern or the Williamsburg Inn. The movie theater was a popular meeting place. First run feature films would change several times a week. A matinee ticket cost only 35 cents. Foreign language films were becoming popular during the Fifties. One afternoon, an Italian film with English subtitles was the featured movie and many of us who did not understand Italian soon knew we were missing much of the film. A number of the football players grew up in homes where Italian was the first spoken language. The players laughed hysterically when the subtitles in some romance scenes would read, "Hello," "How are you," "I am fine," "Isn't is a nice day today," and those of us who didn't understand Italian had to believe the real dialog was either suggestive or profane.

A new slang expression became popular: "Let it all hang out." There were many interpretations and definitions of what it actually meant then, as there are today. Some dictionaries define the phrase as follows: to act or behave without restraint, let go, let loose; to do something enthusiastically and without fear of the results; to relax and do or say exactly what you want to; and to be yourself, assuming that you generally are not; and to become totally relaxed and unpretentious. In the Fifties we each had our own definition for what it meant.

Camel, Chesterfield and Lucky Strike cigarette ads dominated the advertising in *The Flat Hat.* In class, generally the head of the department would teach the freshman entry level course in a subject. At most colleges and universities you will not find the department head in a classroom. Professors never called students by their first names, but always "Mr." or "Miss." The words "political correctness" and "Ms." were not yet in the dictionary. During final exams professors would give out instructions and then tell students and write on the blackboard where they could be found for any questions. There were no monitors or proctors in the classroom during tests or exams. Every student was on his or her honor. During the three-hour exam some students would even take a break and walk to Howard Johnson's for an ice cream cone.

In the Fifties, the campus was surrounded by woods and wetlands which today have become extensions of the campus or new Williamsburg housing developments. The woods were where the students partied when the warmth of Spring blessed the campus. On Saturdays you could always see couples and groups carrying blankets and gallon jugs filled with concocted drinks called "Purple Passion" or "Moose Juice" made from liquor purchased from the state liquor control store on Duke of Gloucester Street. If the clerks checked every student for age the store would probably have had to close for lack of sales. Linwood Cox and Sam Scott, who grew up hunting game around their hometown of Hopewell, Virginia, often went hunting in the woods.

A Football Season Or Not?

Following the Honor Code crisis, Jack Freeman decided not to hold spring football practice. There was concern among the W&M administration, faculty and students whether the college could even field a team that would be able to compete against the teams on the schedule. Freeman had only 15 scholarships and the slashed football budget was not even half the size of the opposing teams. During the summer, William S. "Pappy" Gooch, the business manager of athletics, fielded calls from the athletic directors and his counterparts at the 10 colleges on the schedule. All were worried whether W&M would even have a football team for the 1953 season. They wanted to know if they should try to schedule a last minute replacement for the W&M game. The colleges where W&M would be the visiting team were especially concerned about losing revenue from a home game. Some even suggested that W&M either not compete for a year or schedule games against smaller and much less competitive schools.

In May 1953, seven colleges from the 17-member Southern Conference split to form the new Atlantic Coast Conference. The schools that withdrew were Clemson, Duke, Maryland, North Carolina, North Carolina State, South Carolina, and Wake Forest. Virginia was later added as the eighth conference team. The 10 teams that remained in the Southern Conference in addition to W&M were The Citadel, Davidson, Furman, George Washington, Richmond, Virginia Tech, Virginia Military Institute, Washington & Lee, and West Virginia. Freeman said scheduling difficulties and traveling to some of the schools made it very expensive. The organizers said they wanted to have an eight team pairing for the annual basketball championships at N.C. State's William Neal Reynolds Coliseum in Raleigh that was the conference's major income producer.

Freeman also was athletic director and his salary for both jobs was $6,300. Unlike today, this was a time when university presidents were always the highest paid employee on a campus. He had been a successful high school coach in Pennsylvania when he accepted a job in 1951 to return to W&M as an assistant to Marvin Bass. He and Bass were teammates on the 1942 Southern Conference Championship team that had a 9-1-1 record. Both played together again the next season for the University of Richmond when they were in the Navy V-12 program. From 1939-1950, under coaches Carl Voyles and Rube McCray, W&M had 10 straight winning seasons, won two Southern Conference Championships and played in four post-season bowl games.

A scandal of another kind rocked the campus just two years earlier in the Spring of 1951. High school transcripts for some athletes had been altered so they could meet admissions standards. Dr. John E. Pomfret, the president, McCray, who also was athletic director, Barney Wilson, the head basketball coach and head of the department of physical education, and others resigned.

Following a series of meetings, a special faculty committee wanted more control over all sports. Some administrators, faculty and students even wanted a return to the 1930s era when W&M played only liberal arts colleges with no football subsidy. A significant controversy over the future of football created an ominous dark cloud over not just football, but the entire athletic program.

"This was the beginning of the end of a very successful era of W&M football," said Bill Brink ('54), who played on the 1950 freshman team. "When things began to fall apart that Spring we knew that the football program as we knew it would no longer exist. Nearly half of the 33 players on the team transferred to other colleges. Some didn't come back in the fall because they just could not make it academically. And a number of us were more interested in continuing our education than playing football. Because of the de-emphasis of the program, our scholarships were gone and most of us needed part-time jobs. Before the crisis, you had to be a football player to get a job in the cafeteria. By now it presented a problem if you had played football! I was lucky and did get a job."

Bass had been McCray's line coach and then was an assistant at North Carolina when he returned to W&M as an assistant for the 1950 season. He was named head coach in 1951. He had 75 players on the varsity team and a successful season with 7 wins and 3 losses. After the season and because of the uncertainty of the future of the football program, Bass resigned to be an assistant coach with the Washington Redskins. "The faculty talked about de-emphasis and the administration could not give me any answers," Bass said. Freeman was named to succeed him.

Jack and Jane Freeman had spent their entire life savings to pay the costs of moving from Williamsport, Pennsylvania, to Williamsburg. They lived in a tiny two-bedroom apartment in the college apartments behind Sorority Court. "We were broke," said Jane, "so Jack came home for all of his meals." Both were worried that if the football season was cancelled that Jack might not have a job. The Freemans had two young daughters – Susan, four years old and Patty, three years old – and Jane was pregnant and expecting a third child in December.

Freeman, like many members of his coaching staff and even deans and members of the faculty, had little or no discretionary income. Their social life was limited as was dining out in most Williamsburg restaurants. Many would get together for progressive dinners that were popular among the college's faculty and staff. The evening would start with one family hosting the others for hors d'ouevres. Then the group would go to another residence for the main entrée before ending the evening at yet another for coffee and dessert. And all would bring something to eat or drink.

Football Was Different In the 50s

This was a different era of college football. There were no platoon systems or specialists. Players played both on offense and defense. Quarterbacks called their own plays, did not have "cheat sheets" on their sleeves, held the ball for the place kicker, were on all kickoff and punting teams and after directing the team to a touchdown, would play defense.

Teams did not have 120 players or 85 scholarships like they do today. Freshman not only could not play on the varsity, they could not practice with or scrimmage against the varsity. Freeman's 1952 varsity had 57 players, down from the 75 on Bass' 1951 team. In 1953 he had the challenge of having to field a team with 22 players, a 125-pound kicker and a walk-on who had never played football, even in high school, and with only 15 scholarships.

Players did not have high tech helmets or the padding of today. There were no protective face bars, guards or masks. There were no weight rooms. The positions of a strength and conditioning coach or sports medicine physician did not exist. A full scholarship under NCAA rules included tuition and fees, books, housing, meals and an allowance of $15 a month for laundry and dry cleaning. Few W&M athletes had full scholarships. Every athlete at W&M had a part-time job. Many waited and cleaned tables in the college's cafeteria for their meals. Some worked next door in the Wigwam, a fast-food predecessor to McDonalds. Others had odd jobs from collecting and distributing laundry and dry cleaning to selling sandwiches in the dormitories. A couple of players were even short order cooks. Those in ROTC earned some income for their participation. All needed additional income whether it was for tuition, fees, books, clothes, or spending money.

The First Day of Practice

When the team met for the first time in August, Freeman had 22 players and his 125-pound placekicking specialist Quinby "Hadacol" Hines. The coaching staff consisted of Eric Tipton, Herb "Neepie" Miller, Johnny Clements, Joe Mark and Sonny Cowling. Bill Joyner, the track coach, was the team's trainer, assisted by volunteer Dusty Rhodes, a member of the Williamsburg Fire Department. Rhodes helped by taping the players on game days. Boydson Baird, the head basketball coach, coached the freshman team that had 31 players. Frank Cody was the equipment manager.

Freeman was inspirational and motivational. He instilled a winning spirit in all of the players. As the first practice day was ending, John Risjord, a letterman in track, caught Freeman as he was leaving the field and asked if he could be a walk-on. Risjord apologized for being a day late and said a train wreck between his hometown in Kansas City and Chicago put all trains off schedule. Risjord, who never even played high school football, was encouraged to be a walk-on by Coach Baird, his gym instructor, who sent him a pair of football cleats during the summer.

"I didn't even know how to get into a three-point stance," said Risjord. "I learned from my coaches and teammates." He was "initiated" to the varsity during a practice session when he was knocked out during "light contact" drills. As he was coming to, a teammate who gave him a helping hand, said: "Welcome to the varsity, walk-on."

Freeman had a problem that neither he nor his coaches had faced before – how to scrimmage with so few players. There were not enough players on the team to have a full scrimmage. He knew that there would be even fewer during the season when players were injured. The coaches decided that the only way to make running practice plays work was that when plays were run to the right, the left side of the line would play defense, and when plays were run to the left, the right side of the line would play defense. As the season progressed, often there weren't even enough players physically-able to practice so large blocking and tackling dummies would be used to fill in at certain positions.

"There were a dozen or so very good football players on campus that I played with on our 1950 freshman team," says Charlie Sumner, who quarterbacked the offense, ran, passed, kicked and played defensive safety. "We tried to recruit them as well as good athletes from the intramural six-man touch football league to get walk-ons. There were a number of very good athletes who could have helped us. They all turned us down. But what I remember most, is a player from one of our opponents telling his teammates, 'Guys, they have only 17 players on the team. But those 17 are really players!'" Freeman even spent time in the admissions office scouring freshman applications to see if anyone had played high school football that he might recruit.

Five players were veterans who had been in military service: Jeep Bednarik, Walter "Shorty" Herrmann, Grover "Tommy" Martin, Bill Martin and Jack Place. Tommy Martin and Jack Place played together one season at Camp Lejune, North Carolina. Jim Kelly ('51) remembers that the commanding general at Quantico was recruiting players for his post football team and thought Place was too small to be a starter for his team. "When Lejune played Quantico, Jack scored two touchdowns to beat them," said Kelly. Later Place did play for the Quantico Marines.

"Playing hurt was normal for us that season," remembers Linwood Cox. "Our biggest expenses were the cost of Novocain, adhesive tape, pain killers, hot pads and whatever else was available to keep us going. Teams have tremendous depth today. With the platoon system and specialists it doesn't allow players to even be on the field long enough to be able to experience the phenomena of the second wind."

Al Grieco and George Parozzo both graduated from Barringer High School in Newark, N.J. as did Larry Peccatiello ('58) who played from 1954-1957 and Tony Buccino ('64) who played from 1963-1965. All four captained their teams at Barringer as well as at W&M. Barringer, which was established in 1838, is considered by some to be the third oldest public high school in the country.

W&M 16 - Wake Forest 14

The Indians got off to a great start opening the season with a 16-14 win over Wake Forest before a crowd 17,000 in the Tobacco Bowl in Richmond, Virginia. For the second time in three years, Quinby Hines beat the Demon Deacons. In 1951 his extra point conversion was the 7-6 decision for W&M. This time it was a 17-yard field goal in the last quarter for the margin of victory. Led by Jeep Bednarik's blocking, Bill Bowman broke away for a 71-yard touchdown run in the second quarter. Bednarik did not start because of a sprained ankle but played from the second quarter on. Charlie Sumner's 33-yard run in the final period still left W&M trailing Wake Forest 14-13 until Hines' field goal.

Bowman was named the "Indian of the Week" by *The Flat Hat*. When Bednarik made the key block for Bowman's touchdown run it so infuriated the Wake Forest defender he knocked off his feet that after the play he took a swing at Bednarik and was thrown out of the game. After the game Bednarik went to shake hands with his opponent and show no hard feelings and the player cursed him. Bednarik replied, "Either shake hands or fight." W&M teammates broke it up. Following the game Bednarik's teammates kidded him and Freeman applauded him for his restraint. The Deacon player later played for the Pittsburgh Steelers and following a game against the Philadelphia Eagles asked NFL Hall of Fame lineman Chuck Bednarik, if he was Jeep's older brother. When he responded "yes" the player said, "I owe him one."

W&M 6 - Navy 6

The second week of the season the Indians travelled to Annapolis to face nationally-ranked and highly-favored Navy. The Associated Press ranked the Middies #1 in the East. Navy Coach Eddie Erdelatz had a fresh, new team start the second quarter hoping to wear-down and tire W&M. After a scoreless first half, Navy took a 6-0 lead in the third quarter. Early in the fourth quarter Al Grieco recovered a Navy fumble and following an unnecessary roughness penalty against Navy, threw a 15-yard touchdown pass to Tommy Martin to tie the game. A fumbled snap from center foiled Hines' attempted point after kick and he was tackled trying to run it the end zone for the lead. W&M had another opportunity with 2:30 left in the game. Hines attempted a difficult angle field goal from the 17 but it was blocked by the Navy defense.

The W&M defense shut down Navy quarterback George Welsh, who went on to be a legendary coach at University of Virginia and be elected to the College Football Hall of Fame. The W&M offensive line neutralized Steve "Ike" Eisenhauer, Navy's All-American lineman. *Life* magazine reported the story with pictures of a jubilant Iron Indian team celebrating the 6-6 tie in the locker room, Jeep Bednarik holding his two-year-old son, and Freeman wiping away tears from his eyes after co-captains Tommy Martin and Steve Milkovich presented him with the game ball.

There were more injuries during the game – Jerry Sazio and Charlie Copeland both with knees and Aubrey Fitzgerald with a broken nose. After the game, Sazio pulled a ring out of the watch pocket in his blue jeans and proposed to his girlfriend and cheerleader, Dot Bailey. Bill Marfizo, who had his helmet dented when he was kicked in the head nearly blocking a punt, played seven different positions during the game. A sports reporter nicknamed him "Mr. Versatility." Al Grieco was named "Indian of the Week."

Cincinnati 57 - W&M 7

Based on the first two games, the Las Vegas odds makers made W&M a two touchdown favorite over powerhouse Cincinnati, a team that lost only one game the previous season and were defending Mid-America Conference champions. Coach Sid Gillman, considered the inventor of the two-platoon and the "West Coast Offense," took advantage of the injury-riddled Iron Indians during the night game in Cincinnati. Gillman had players three-deep at every position and the Bearcats quickly had a 20-0 first quarter lead. Knee injuries limited playing time for Jerry Sazio, George Parozzo and several others. Merciless, Gilman kept yelling for his team to "pour it on" and following a fourth quarter touchdown and 50-7 lead, he even tried an onsides kickoff. Charlie Sumner, who scored the only W&M touchdown, was named "Indian of the Week."

On the charter flight home, Freeman asked for all the injured to sit in the back of the plane to be treated by trainer Bill Joyner. John Risjord responded, "I don't think there's enough room back here, coach." To take away the sting of defeat and have some fun, Aubrey Fitzgerald and other players tricked Eric Tipton into turning up his hearing aid. The players walked by him mouthing words and when he turned it up to full volume, all of the players let out a yell. The team had a well deserved week off after the loss.

W&M 13 - Virginia Tech 7

After three weeks on the road, the Iron Indians were happy to return to Cary Field and treated a sellout, standing-room-only home crowd of 12,500 to a 13-7 victory over Virginia Tech. The passing and running of Charlie Sumner and running of Bill Bowman provided the offense. The defense was outstanding. VPI was only in W&M territory once in the first half and that because of a recovered fumble.

Early in the second quarter Sumner got things started by returning a punt from his 28 yard line to the 43. He then directed a drive to the eight where Bowman scored on two running plays. The first half ended with W&M on the 17-yard line and leading 7-0. Late in the third quarter Sumner directed an 80-yard drive with Bowman again scoring on a short run. VPI was scoreless until 3:58 remaining in the game when a 35-yard drive, started by a recovered W&M fumble, put them in the game. An earlier drive of 73 yards ended when the Gobblers could not score on four tries from the W&M two-yard line. With only seconds left in the game, VPI was threatening again when Tommy Martin intercepted Johnny Dean's pass on the eight.

For the second straight game, Charlie Sumner was named "Indian of the Week." By this time of the season, Bill Martin and Jerry Sazio had their own signaling system when certain running plays would be called. "I played left halfback and Jerry was at left tackle," Martin recalls. "When we had an off tackle dive play where I would be driving straight ahead, once Jerry could size up the defensive alignment and who he was going to block, he would signal me. He would wiggle his right foot if he was going to block the defensive lineman to the right and vice versa with his left foot. It almost always worked so I had a clear shot through the line for a gain."

W&M 12 - George Washington 7

Charlie Sumner scored the winning touchdown and intercepted a pass on the last play of the game to preserve a Homecoming victory. Just two minutes into the final quarter, Sumner ran four yards off left tackle for the go-ahead touchdown that was set up by a 38-yard kickoff return by Bill Bowman. After stopping a GW drive on the 22 and with time running out in the first half, Sumner engineered a nine-play, 78-yard drive that ended with Shorty Herrmann scoring from the three to give W&M 6-0 halftime lead.

The Colonials had a first down on the nine with 1:31 left in the game when Sumner intercepted a fourth down pass in the end zone to clinch the win. Entering the game, GW had the third best passing offense in the country. GW Coach Bob Sherman freely used his bench and substituted to great advantage to try and wear down W&M.

During the halftime ceremonies, Admiral Alvin Duke Chandler, W&M president, crowned the Homecoming Queen, Barbara Crosset ('54), a senior from Swarthmore, Pennsylvania, and a member of Kappa Alpha Theta sorority. She would become Mrs. William Brink ('54). The dance theme was pink and blue champagne. Art Mooney and his orchestra provided the music. George Parozzo was named "Indian of the Week."

W&M 7 - North Carolina State 6

Aubrey Fitzgerald broke through the Wolfpack line to block Al D'Angelo's extra point attempt and preserve a 7-6 win for W&M, its fourth of the season. After a scoreless first half, W&M took the second half kickoff and drove 70 yards with Bill Bowman scoring on an eight-yard run. Quinby Hines' extra point was the margin of victory.

N. C. State recovered four W&M fumbles and intercepted two passes to stop several scoring drives. The outstanding Iron Indian defense stopped the Wolfpack several times inside the red zone. For his exceptional play on both offense and defense, Jeep Bednarik was voted the "Indian of the Week."

VMI 20 - W&M 19

A 23-yard touchdown pass from Dave Woolwine to Johnny Mapp with only 56 seconds left gave Virginia Military Institute a 20-19 upset win. Playing in near freezing weather in Roanoke, the Keydets marched 70 yards in the last three minutes to score and ruin the Indians' chances for a share of the Southern Conference and Big Six championships as well as a possible post-season bowl invitation. Only 5,000 fans braved the cold for the third annual Shrine classic.

The game was only seven minutes old when Charlie Sumner scored after a short drive for a 6-0 lead. But then a lost fumble and an intercepted pass led to two VMI touchdowns for a 14-6 halftime lead. W&M took the second half kickoff and in 1:20 had marched 77 yards for a touchdown behind the running of Sumner, Bill Bowman, Bob Elzey and Shorty Herrmann. Before the period had ended, W&M had a 19-14 lead.

For the first time this season, an opposing team used fewer players than W&M. VMI played only 15 men compared to 17 Iron Indians. For the second time this season Bill Bowman was named "Indian of the Week."

W&M 21 - Richmond 0

The Iron Indians lost no time in recovering from the VMI loss. On the first play of the game Bill Marfizo recovered a Spiders' fumble on the 46 and five plays later Bill Bowman scored. W&M scored on drives of 60 and 39 yards in the second half while the defense held Richmond scoreless. A Richmond Homecoming crowd of 18,000 was hoping to break a string of losses to W&M that dated back to 1938.

Richmond threatened twice driving to within yards of the end zone, but W&M recovered a fumble on the two-yard line and intercepted a pass on the eight to preserve the shutout. For his outstanding effort on both offense and defense Chet Waksmunski, the youngest player on the team at 18, was voted "Indian of the Week."

Washington & Lee 33 - W&M 7

With Charlie Sumner sidelined because of an ankle injury, W&M could not sustain the offense it had against Richmond. In the third quarter, Sumner hobbled off the bench to throw a 28-yard touchdown pass to Shorty Herrmann. Quinby Hines' extra point tied the game at 7-7. However, W&L's Carl Bolt returned the ensuing kickoff 92 yards for a touchdown taking the spirit out of the 3,000 Indian fans in attendance. The Generals went on to score after an intercepted pass and a blocked punt on the next two series. The Iron Indians could never recover. Shorty Herrmann was named "Indian of the Week."

Boston University 41 - W&M 14

Playing before the smallest home crowd of the season, only 2,500. the injury-riddled Iron Indians stopped Boston University on its first drive, but then could not contain the Terriers. BU took a 14-0 lead in the first quarter, scored three more times in the third quarter and again in the final period. W&M could not get past the Terriers' 37-yard line until late in the game. W&M lacked its offensive power with Sumner still ailing and lost three fumbles and had two passes intercepted. Almost every Iron Indian was playing with some type of injury.

Because of the Thanksgiving holiday *The Flat Hat* sportswriters did not select an "Indian of the Week."

After a magnificent and unexpected start, losing only once in its first six games, W&M ended the season with a 5-4-1 record. Injuries were too much to overcome. The following season, the 1954 team had a 4-4-2 record. It would not be until 1965, in Marv Levy's second season as head football coach, before W&M had another winning season, 6-4.

Campus Love

This was an era when many college romances blossomed into life long partnerships. William and Mary was no different. Several of the Iron Indians married their campus sweethearts. Aubrey Fitzgerald and Shirley Richardson. Jerry Sazio and Dot Bailey. Tommy Martin and Katherine Bell. Charlie Copeland and Charlene Foster. Linwood Cox and Shelly Jane Bailey. Quinby Hines and Ann Callihan. Shorty Herrmann and Tish Rustad. Doug Henley and Barbara Ann Pharo. Even Jack and Jane Freeman met as students at W&M. This was true also of many basketball players and those who contributed to this book. Al Kersey and Joann Lore. Jerry Harris and Ann Johnson. Joe Agee and Eloise Bryant. Pete Crenier and Sandy Bettiger. Bill Brink and Barbara Crosset. Jim Kelly and Bev Simonton. Jim Kaplan and Jane Thompson.

Many of the first meetings of the couples took place in and around Jockey Corner. Linwood Cox remembers meeting his future wife, Shelly Bailey, inside the Corner Greek's restaurant at Jockey Corner when they were introduced by teammate Shorty Herrmann. Aubrey Fitzgerald says the first time he met Shirley Richardson he was sitting on the steps of the Methodist Church at Jockey Corner praying that God would deliver him a date. "I then detected the enticing smell of cookies and candy in a package Shirley's father in Suffolk had her," he said. "She was walking from the post office to her Brown Hall dorm. I asked her if he could join her. When she said 'yes' I said to myself 'My prayers have been answered.'" That was the start of a romance that continued in a biology class lab and baby sitting. They were babysitters for Jack and Jane Freeman, paid 35 cents an hour and had to bring their own snacks. Aubrey remembers the first time he went to get something to eat and the Freemans' refrigerator and cupboards were bare. He had a part-time job picking up laundry from several dormitories and probably had more discretionary spending money than his coach.

Aubrey broke his nose in the Navy game and Freeman turned down his request to wear a face guard. "Only chickens wear face guards!," he said. When he was thrown out of the Cincinnati game for hitting the quarterback, Freeman said "Only cowards leave games that way." Aubrey responded, "But coach, I was the only one out there fighting."

Card games, especially bridge, were popular at the time. Tish Rustad remembers that Short Herrmann would drop by Brown Hall for pickup games of bridge in the dormitory parlor. This is where they first met. Their first date was on St. Patrick's Day of 1954 at a green beer party at the Kappa Sigma Lodge.

Fun and Jokes

"Practical jokes were common among the guys on the team," said Linwood Cox. "We all would put a self-addressed penny post card in the Blue Book so the professor could mail us our final exam grade along with the final semester grade. When I picked up the mail and a card for one course where I went into the exam with a solid B+ average it was marked D-. I ran over to the professor's house to confront him and he just laughed and said: 'Your buddies have played a trick on you.' My final grade was a B."

Eric Tipton had just retired from professional baseball and became a fulltime coach at W&M. He was one of the greatest punters in college football and in 1965 was elected to the College Football Hall of Fame. A very personable individual, he was loved and respected by all of the players. He was hearing impaired and needed to wear a hearing aid with a bulky battery pack. This made him a target for pranks by the players who would jokingly mouth words or questions, let him turn up his hearing aid, and then shout at him. Bill Tucker ('58), who was on the freshman team, recalls seeing Bob Elzey run off the field after a late practice and jump an imaginary fence. "Tip had to check it out and looked around for a wire that just wasn't there. Realizing he was the subject of a prank, he said 'That boy isn't all there!'"

Aubrey Fitzgerald was known for his fun, comic relief and hijinx. The following year W&M team played West Virginia University in Morgantown. Travel was not easy then. There was no budget to charter an airplane for a flight. The first leg of the trip was a bus ride to Washington, D.C., then the train to Connellsville, Pennsylvania, followed by a bus ride to the destination. The team was in one Pullman sleeper car with upper and lower berths. In the middle of the night, the train stopped because a freight train had derailed on an adjacent track. The train moved forward, stopped, then back, and repeated the moves several times, waking a number of sleeping players. Aubrey got up from his berth to stretch and walk up and down the aisle. At one end of the coach he saw the conductor's jacket and hat. Many of the awakened players looked out from behind the berth curtains as he entertained them wearing the conductor's uniform. As Aubrey was saying, "All aboard … all aboard," he was unaware that Freeman was right behind him, until he said, "If you don't get back into bed immediately, I'll put you on a bus home." Everyone broke out laughing when he responded, "But Coach, I don't work buses."

Jerry Sazio and Dot Bailey

Jerry Sazio and Dot Bailey became engaged after the Navy game when he gave her a ring that he pulled from the watch pocket of his Levis. He was a champion bridge player who competed in tournaments and they often played bridge at the Pi Beta Phi house with her sorority sisters. She was a cheerleader and the 1952 homecoming queen. As a high school standout in New Jersey, Jerry was widely recruited by colleges including Vanderbilt, Kansas, the U.S. Military Academy and Virginia, but decided to follow his brother Ralph to W&M. His future wife also helped him in mid-season when Freeman wanted him to be ready to kick extra points. She held the ball for him while he practiced and her sorority sisters would help by retrieving the kicked balls. "I was always afraid he was going to kick me," said Dot, "so I couldn't look."

During one summer school session he had to withdraw to care for his mother who was dying of Leukemia. She needed to be driven several times a week to New York City for treatment at Sloane-Kettering Cancer Center. Both of his parents were Italian, his father was deceased, and Jerry says that the only word in English his mother knew was an expletive – s***. While at home, he had a part-time job driving a truck for the Murchison family jewelry business that also made the W&M college class rings and the engagement ring for his future wife.

Because of his mother's illness, he missed several econ classes. Dr. Tony Sancetta called him in and told him a story. "When you go to the zoo and look at the monkeys, you can't tell one from another or know if one is missing," said the professor. "However, when you go to see the elephants, if one is missing, you know it!" Dr. Sancetta also congratulated Sazio for an A-grade paper on "The Economic Integration Of Europe As A Third World Power." Sazio said he chose the subject because of his Italian heritage and believed the countries of Europe would someday need to unite to keep pace with the U.S. and Russia. Today Jerry's vision has become the European Union of 27 sovereign states.

Charlie Copeland and Charlene Foster

Charlie Copeland, who also was called "Hump" during his W&M days, remembers the first time he saw his future wife, Charlene Foster. "I finished football practice, just had dinner and was standing at the Wren Building courtyard entrance on Jockey Corner with a group of other players checking out the females in the freshman class returning from the post office to their dorms. Charlene was a house monitor at Ludwell and was shepherding 15 or so freshman around," he said. "My teammates started harassing the coeds and didn't realize Charlene was an upper classman. I could see that this bothered her and when I told them to stop, they did. I then walked with her to the shuttle bus for the Ludwell dormitories and learned she was no longer dating a friend of mine. Within a week we began dating and our relationship developed."

Charlie says his relationship with Charlene changed his life. Rather than play cards with buddies or go to a movie, he would go with her to the library to study. Charlene was on the Dean's List and as a result, his grades improved significantly because of his new study habits just being with her. The two started going to church regularly. "In the 1954 game against Navy, just before halftime, my knee popped as I was chasing Joe Gattusso around left end. Surgery the following week ended my playing days," he said. "Charlene visited me as I convalesced in the college Infirmary. By Christmas we shared dreams and talked about a future together. In those days if you wanted to marry someone, you first asked permission from the father," Charlie added. So before the two became engaged on Valentine's Day he first went home with her to Lynchburg to ask her father's permission.

Charlie held several part-time jobs including picking up and delivery laundry for two men's dormitories – Old Dominion and Monroe Halls – and working the counter at Howard Johnson's and Danny Matola's Greek restaurant. His cousin, Robert Wallace, owned the local hardware store and sometimes would hire him to install linoleum tile. As a marketing major he interviewed with various companies for a job and General Electric hired him for their Business Training Program. He was able to delay for a year reporting for active military duty at Ft. Sill which he believes help solidify his career.

Nicknames and Anecdotes

Many of the players had nicknames. No one is certain exactly how they originated or whether any particular individual was responsible. John Bednarik was "Jeep." Charlie

Copeland was "Hump." Quinby Hines was "Hadacol."[1] Walter Herrmann was "Shorty." Bill Martin was Wiz. Linwood Cox was "Skinny Linny" because he weighed only 178 pounds. Charlie Sumner was called "Raincoat" because he always wore a raincoat, regardless of the weather, rain or sunshine or season of the year. This was nearly 20 years before Peter Falk has his signature raincoat for his Columbo television character.

Sumner and Cox worked part-time picking up and delivering dry-cleaning for a local cleaner and were paid 50 percent of the proceeds. Cox remembers one entrepreneur in Old Dominion dormitory who had a hot-dog machine and a profitable business selling them on weekends. One summer Sumner worked as a short order cook at Howard Johnson's and another year he was a clerk at the state controlled liquor store. Jeep Bednarik worked for the Colonial Williamsburg Maintenance Department. Bill Bowman and others worked during the summer season at *The Common Glory* in a variety of jobs. Many of the players worked in the cafeteria or The Wigwam or local restaurants.

Co-captain Steve Milkovich was known as "Weed." Weed was not known then for what it is today – marijuana. In fact, there was none. He held down several part time jobs including selling soft drinks at dances. "Few of us had any spending money and I do remember I could always go to the Wigwam and get a grilled cheese sandwich for only 25 cents," he said. Not only did he have problems with both knees but he went through the entire '53 season with a cut on the bridge of his nose that would not heal. "Getting it taped and bandaged did no good," he adds. "In a game after a couple of plays and with no face guard, any bandage would come off. The only thing I could do to stop the bleeding was rub dirt on it." In the final game of the season against Boston University he was kicked in the mouth while making a tackle. It drove his teeth through his bottom lip and after the game he was sent to the infirmary for stitches.

"When the season was over I was sent to Richmond to see a specialist about my nose," Milkovich adds. "By this time there was a growth inside my lower lip that concerned me. I asked the doctor to please do something about it. He said he was being paid only for the nose, but called Coach Freeman to double check. He said Freeman's response was 'No … we don't have the money and that would only be cosmetic.'" Doctors determined his knees showed "evidence of calcification of the attachment of the medial collateral ligament on the femur with some traumatic arthritic changes in the knees." This cost him a commission in the U.S. Marines and a medical discharge.

No one dared nickname George Parozzo. He had the stereotype looks, size and demeanor of a member of the New Jersey Mafia and to be cast in *The Godfather* or *The Sopranos*. "George was actually a very shy person," said Jerry Sazio, who roomed with him for a year. "He was the complete opposite of the image and personality that he projected. He was a very good student but he didn't want people to know how intelligent he was. In a way, he was like a gentle giant and not the out-going type. If you were a friend, he would do absolutely anything for you."

---

[1] In the late 1940s and during the 1950s, Hadacol was a popular medicine promoted as a dietary and vitamin supplement that was a cure all for any ailment. It also had 12 percent alcohol and was very popular in the dry counties of many Southern States.

Gordon Vliet remembers sitting behind Parozzo in an econ class and watching him mark up *The Daily Racing Form* folded behind the business section of the newspaper which faced the professor. "While George would sometimes sit on the bench on Jamestown Road, Jockey Corner was his forum for harassing and intimidating coeds and underclassmen," says Bill Tucker.

Many Iron Indians flew in an airplane for the first time that year. Charlie Copeland remembers the team boarding a plane in Richmond in a blinding snowstorm to fly to Cincinnati. "There was absolute silence on the plane. Many of us were scared. All we could see outside was white," Copeland said. "And then, from the back of the plane I heard a small voice in a whisper say, 'Let's sing a church song.' It was George Parozzo. And then he began singing a song popular at the time, 'Crying in the Chapel.'"

Bill Tucker says another player who loved to sing was Al Grieco. "My brother Turk (Charles Tucker '58) roomed with him for three years. He had a 45 rpm player and loved to sing Italian songs along with Frank Sinatra, Tony Bennett and Tony Martin. You could hear him throughout the dorm! Bro Turk shared many stories of visits with Al's family, particularly the multiple-course Italian Sunday dinners and an afternoon at the table."

A number of athletes would sit on the bench on Jamestown Road near the Morris House dormitory. "That's where Quinby and I first met when I was walking from Barrett Dorm to either the post office or cafeteria," said Ann Callihan. "Quinby and I got even better acquainted in Dr. Carter's Spanish class, especially when I helped him with homework and before any tests or exams. The one person whose looks and size really terrified us was George Parozzo. If he was sitting on the bench we would walk across the street to avoid walking on the sidewalk past him because he was so intimidating."

A Very Tight Budget

"The athletic department budget was so tight we could hardly afford to send out news releases to promote players for all-conference or all-American honors or to even build attendance at home games," said Rene A. Henry, who was athletic press secretary. The title of his predecessors had been sports information director but was changed by Admiral Chandler. "I had no budget to take trips to speak at sports clubs in even Norfolk or Richmond much less to make long distance telephone calls to sportswriters to build support for the team and players. I had no money for a photographer to take publicity photos. But the athletic department owned a bulky Speed Graphic camera that used 4"x5" film that I used to take all of the publicity photos. I then had to develop the film and make the prints in a photo lab in the fine arts department."

Henry recalls an incident that took place one evening after dinner in the athletic offices in Blow Gymnasium. "I was writing news releases on an old manual typewriter, cutting stencils and duplicating them on a mimeograph machine. Several of my fraternity brothers were earning either 35 cents or 50 cents an hour folding them, stuffing them in pre-addressed envelopes and adding postage stamps.

"I worked in a corner of a large room opposite from Pappy Gooch. Jack Freeman had come back to his office following dinner. Marshall Ries asked me why we were mailing the news releases second class mail since some may not get to a newspaper in time to be used before a game. I told him that was all we could afford because of the budget and that the mailings were targeted and limited, making it difficult to promote players for any all-conference, all-state and all-American honors.

"Then, in his Boston/Harvard accent, Marshall replied: 'Well, it only costs a penny more to go first class!'" The next afternoon when I was working at my desk Jack Freeman, who had overhead the conversation, came to me and said in the future to send out all news releases first class."

Excitement In the Burg – A Panty Raid

During this time, about the most exciting thing that happened on campus that year was a beer can barricade built across Richmond Road to protest some action taken by Admiral Chandler regarding the fraternity lodges. It was easily and quickly removed the next morning by campus personnel and no one was hurt and there wasn't any damage.

The W&M campus had yet to have a panty raid which seemed to be the rage at many colleges throughout the country. One warm, Fall evening, several Sigma Alpha Epsilon fraternity brothers were hanging out at Jockey Corner and enthusiastically appreciating the passing coeds. They were approached by several Shriners who were in town for a conference. The Shriners asked the SAEs what happened in town or on campus for excitement. As the conversation developed, the Fez-wearing Shriners suggested a panty raid. They promised to provide beer to the SAEs if they would organize the event and involve other fraternities. This suggestion was met with approval, and strategy and organization immediately commenced.

The students then called their fraternity brother, Gene Guess, who had the campus beer concession with Joe Cardaci, also an SAE. Both were from the Washington, D.C. metropolitan area. Guess, who went on to become a successful lawyer and speaker of the legislature in Alaska, needed Cardaci because he was 21 years old. Also, Joe had a 1937 Packard given to him a year earlier by his uncle. When the back seat was removed, the car could carry some 40 cases and several kegs of beer. "Gene and I were the only ones on campus who knew how to tap a keg," said Cardaci, "so we got invited to a lot of parties." Joe was a high school all-American and started on the 1949 and 1950 W&M football teams. He then served on active duty in the military but was not eligible to play when returned to campus in 1953, and graduated in 1954.

That evening Sandy Bettiger (Crenier) and Mary Meyers (Vitale) were in their first floor room in Barrett Women's Dormitory when they heard voices in the bushes outside of their room. Someone asked them to go to the end of the hall and unlock and open the side doors to let them in. "We looked out the window, a crowd was gathering, and someone was blowing "charge" on a bugle," Sandy remembers. "As the group gathering at the dormitory's main entrance swelled, Dean Lambert (J. Wilfred Lambert, Dean of

Students) blocked the doors. Then the crowed switched their attention to the end doors of the dormitory which were being guarded by Dean Joe Farrar (Joe Farrar, Dean of Men).

"The hallways were filled with girls running back and forth. Others were leaning out of second and third floor windows taunting the fraternity boys. The bugle kept sounding charge," she continued. "Finally Dean Lambert decided one way to get the men back to their rooms and restore calm on the campus, was to offer them a walk through the first floor of the dorm. He insisted on order and told the girls to stay in their rooms and keep their doors shut. He led the men to the side door intending to parade them down the hall, through the main lobby, and out the other end of the building.

"By the time the first men in the group reached half the length of the hall, a large number of them had peeled off the end and ran up the end stair case to the upper floors. You could hear girls yelling 'Man on the floor … man on the floor' and doors slamming shut. When the rest of the mean realized what was happening, they too dashed up the center stairwell to the upper floors to join their fellow students.

"After a while, the two deans left matters in the hands of the housemother and decided to walk over to Tyler Annex, a small men's dormitory on the other side of campus, hoping to find some of the ring leaders and instigators there," remembers Sandy.

No one can recall if the known perpetrators of the raid received any disciplinary action other than strongly worded, individually issued warnings. There was no property damage and no one was injured. Louis Lambert Kale, now W&M's executive director of The Historic Campus, remembers as a young child how her father, the Dean, was called that night about the panty raid. "We lived on Jamestown Road across from Barrett and my brother and I looked out of our bedroom windows and could hear the excitement, but all of the action was taking place on the side of the building that faced the Sunken Gardens.

The Season Finale

The College held a special convocation on Friday, December 11 to honor the Iron Indians. The tribute grew out of a spontaneous desire of the faculty, student body and administration to honor the team. The event took place in old Phi Beta Kappa Hall before a packed audience of fans, friends, faculty and alumni. "We backed them all season and we think they did a great job," said Cary Scates, president of the student body, who acted as the master of ceremonies. "This has been one of the best years in the football history of the school," said Admiral Alvin Duke Chandler, W&M president.

"Pappy Gooch" presented every member of the team and the coaching staff with individual commemorative scrolls signed by Scates for the student body; Chandler for the administration; Dr. Charles Marsh, Dean of the Faculty; and W. Stirling King for the Society of the Alumni. The seven seniors also were given gold wrist watches.

In addition to remarks by Scates, Chandler, and Marsh, others who spoke included Jim Barnes, Secretary of the Alumni; Hugh DeSamper representing the W&M Educational

Foundation; Mel Hines, vice president of the student body; and Jack Freeman and co-captains Tommy Martin and Steve Milkovich. The band, choir and cheerleaders added to the festivities.

The next morning Jane Freeman gave birth to Michael.

The special convocation was the last event held in Phi Beta Kappa Hall. During the Christmas holidays it was destroyed by fire.

Rene A. Henry (W&M '54)
August 2011

Roster of Players

Player/Position	Class	No.	Age	Height	Weight	Hometown
John "Jeep" Bednarik, E	'54	17	25	6'0"	215	Bethlehem, Penn.
*Bill Bowman, FB	'54	24	21	6'2"	205	Birmingham, Ala.
Charles Copeland, T	'55	57	20	6'0"	225	Hampton, Va.
Linwood Cox, G	'55	54	21	6"0"	180	Hopewell, Va.
*Bob Elzey, HB/QB	'55	14	21	5'10"	170	Salisbury, Md.
Aubrey Fitzgerald, G	'56	78	20	6'0"	190	Waynesboro, Va.
*Al Grieco, QB/HB	'56	71	20	5'8"	160	Newark, N.J.
*Doug Henley, FB	'57	12	19	6'0"	187	South Norfolk, Va.
*Shorty Herrmann, HB	'55	26	24	5'10"	170	Warwick, Va.
*L.Q. Hines, PK	'55	11	21	5'8"	125	Suffolk, Va.
*George Karschner, HB	'56	30	18	6'0"	200	Williamsport, Penn.
Bill Marfizo, C/E/LB	'56	76	18	6'2"	194	Windber, Penn.
William "Bill" Martin, HB	'55	10	23	5'10"	180	Linden, N.J.
*Tommy Martin, HB/E	'54	23	24	5'11"	205	Roanoke, Va.
Steve Milkovich, C/G	'54	47	22	5'11"	195	Johnstown, Penn.
*Bill Nagy, G/T	'56	63	20	5'11"	180	Baker Whitely, Penn.
*George Parozzo, T	'54	90	22	6'2"	235	Newark, N.J.
*Jack Place, HB	'54	15	23	5'11"	175	Spencerville, Ohio
Bill Riley, E	'56	55	19	5'11"	160	Holsopple, Penn.
John Risjord, E	'55	79	20	6'2"	170	Kansas City, Mo.
Jerry Sazio, T/G/LB	'55	37	20	6'0"	220	Irvington, N.J.
*Sam Scott, T	'55	56	21	6'2"	200	Hopewell, Va.
Charlie Sumner, QB/HB	'55	21	22	6'1"	185	Salem, Va.
*Chet Waksmunski, G/T	'56	83	18	6'1"	197	Hastings, Penn.

*Deceased

The Schedule

September 19, Richmond, Va.	W&M 16	Wake Forest 14
September 26, Annapolis, Md.	W&M 6	Navy 6
October 3, Cincinnati, Ohio	Cincinnati 57	W&M 7
October 17, Williamsburg	W&M 13	Virginia Tech 7
October 24, Williamsburg	W&M 12	George Washington 7
October 31, Raleigh, N.C.	W&M 7	North Carolina St. 6
November 7, Roanoke, Va.	VMI 20	W&M 19
November 14, Richmond	W&M 21	Richmond 0
November 21, Williamsburg	W&L 33	W&M 7
November 28, Williamsburg	Boston Univ. 41	W&M 14

The 24 Iron Indians

The following profiles of the 24 Iron Indians are reprinted from the 1953 William & Mary Football Handbook that was published for the media. Following the publication's description is a summary of the professional career of each. In 1979 the Iron Indians team was inducted in the W&M Sports Hall of Fame. Several also have been inducted as individuals for their exceptional performance and success.

   Deceased

John "Jeep" Bednarik – Senior, 25, 6'0", 215 - Bethlehem, Penn. (1928-   )

Is the younger brother of Penn's famous all-American, Chuck Bednarik. "Jeep" is a sturdy, rugged competitor. He is an outstanding defensive end and will be a stalwart flankman this season. He will be hard to stop as a pass receiver with his 6', 215-pound frame driving him on. He excelled on the track team last spring throwing the shot put and discus. A physical education major, he hopes to play professional football upon graduation. He is married and has a two-year-old son he hopes will grow up to be just like his father.

Before enrolling at William & Mary he served two years in the U.S. Navy, 18 months of which were in the South Pacific. He was honored for his efforts during the '53 season and named honorable mention on the United Press all-America team and first team all-State (Virginia) on both the AP and UPI teams. He signed with the Baltimore Colts as a free agent. After graduation he taught and coached at Gloucester (Virginia) High School for one year before moving to Easton (Pennsylvania) High School as assistant football coach and to teach physical education.

After five years Jeep became head coach and teacher of health and physical education a Neptune (New Jersey) High School. During his six years at Neptune the team won the Shore Conference Championship and was ranked #6 in the state. He moved back to Pennsylvania to be head coach at Louis E. Dieruff High School in Allentown. After six years, he became an assistant football coach for 13 years at Lehigh University in his hometown of Bethlehem. When he thought he had retired, because of his love of football he was lured back to coaching a ninth grade team for another six years in Emmaus. He and his wife Mary live in Allentown, have a son and daughter. Teammate Jerry Sazio is the Godfather of his son.

* Bill Bowman – Senior, 21, 6'2", 205 - Birmingham, Ala. (1932-2008)

Terrific runner, good pass receiver, excellent blocker, good passer, frequent scorer – these qualities make Bill Bowman William & Mary's 1953 candidate for all-America honors. "Bullet Bill," as his teammates tab him because of his elusive speed, is the Big Green's greatest running fullback since Jack Cloud. An outfielder on the baseball team, he has exceptionally fast speed for his size and can break 11.0 seconds in full equipment in the 100-yard dash. Last season he averaged 6.1 yards per try gaining 571 yards on 93 carries. He is an excellent blocker, both leading interference and downfield. He picked up a few more tricks of the trade and displayed a dynamic running stride in spring drills. A business administration major, he is concentrating on accounting. He is a member of the Accounting Club, Scabbard & Blade, Varsity Club and Lambda Chi Alpha fraternity. He'll be a sure bet for all-sectional honors and a top candidate for all-America.

Bowman was named honorable mention on both the Associated Press and United Press all-America teams, first team all-Southern Conference and first team all-State (Virginia) on both AP and UPI teams. He was honored to play in the North-South game in Miami and played fullback on offense and linebacker on defense. He was the second draft choice of the Detroit Lions and was the starting fullback the 1954 season. In 12 games he rushed 96 times for 397 yards, an average of 4.1 per carry, caught 34 passes for 288 yards and returned 12 kicks for 178 yards, an average of 29.7 yards each time. He then fulfilled his military service commitment as a field artillery officer. When he returned to the Lions in 1956 he never regained the form he had as a starting rookie and finished his career in 1957 with the Pittsburgh Steelers.

Bill earned his law degree from the University of Tennessee and served as a U.S. prosecutor for the U.S. Attorney's Office. He was a defense lawyer for 30 years in Greenville, Tennessee and then was assistant district attorney for 17 years prior to his retirement in 2006. He was active in numerous civic organizations. He was a duplicate bridge fanatic and awarded the distinction for Master Bridge Player in Tennessee in 2007. He was inducted into the W&M Sports Hall of fame in 1972 and again in 1979 as a member of the Iron Indians team. He lived in Greenville, Tennessee with his wife Dee Dee and has three sons.

Charles Copeland – Junior, 20, 6"0", 225 - Hampton, Va. (1933-   )

Was hampered last year by a bad knee, but should come around after an operation. "Humphrey" as he is nicknamed, was a defensive whiz for Hampton High prior to coming to W&M. Solid as a rock in the line, he needs more speed to go both ways. He is a nephew of Watson Copeland, who captained the 1919 Tribe team. A business administration major, he is a member of Sigma Nu fraternity.

After graduation he worked for General Electric in the financial management training program. When he completed officer training at Ft. Sill, Oklahoma he was assigned to an armored artillery division in Baumholder, Germany. Charlie relocated to Frankfurt as

Aide-de-Camp to Brig. Gen. James W. Holsinger. After two years he rejoined General Electric. In 1958 he became a special agent with Prudential Insurance Agency in Newport News. A year later he joined Old Point National Bank in Phoebus. In 1963 he was lured to the financial department of Honeywell and relocated to Largo, Florida.

In 1960 he was recruited by Radiation, Inc./Harris Corporation in Melbourne, Florida where he worked for 19 years involved in production control and finance. It meant moves to Miami, Quincy, Illinois, and Los Angeles. When he lived in Illinois he had frequent week-long trips to California's Silicone Valley to indoctrinate companies to his organization. Charlie was promoted from one division to another and when he was managing a worldwide system of radio and television broadcast systems he spent time in Saudi Arabia, Indonesia, Nigeria and Liberia. In 1987 he became president of Belfort Instrument Company in Baltimore, Maryland where he retired three years later. His wife is the former Charlene Foster ('56) and they live in Broomfield, Colorado.

Linwood Cox – Junior, 21, 6"0", 180 – Hopewell, Va. (1932-)

"Little Lindy" as he has been aptly tabbed because of his size, is a sprinter in track, and like a package of dynamite to his opposition. He has been a starter for two years since entering William & Mary. Last year he was named to the Associated Press all-America team (honorable mention) and first team all-Southern Conference. He will more than likely be named to many more all-star teams in the future. Was a teammate of Sam Scott in high school where together they led Hopewell to several state championships. He is hailed as another Garrard "Buster" Ramsey because of his swiftness, ability, and know-how, and has lived up to that reputation thus far. An economics major, he is a member of Kappa Sigma fraternity.

In 1953 season, he was named to the Associated Press' second team all-State (Virginia). In 1952 he was named all-Southern Conference and honorable mention all-America by AP. After graduation he completed his officers' training course at Quantico and was commissioned a second lieutenant in the U.S. Marine Corp. Linwood wore the same tuxedo which was the prize his senior year for being chosen "Mr. Formal" when he married the former Shelly Jane Bailey ('55). They were married in Washington, D.C. at the Walter Reed base chapel where Shelly had been baptized and her father, an Army doctor, was stationed at the hospital.

The Marines sent him to Tyndal Air Force Base, Florida for radar air-controller training for two months and then assigned him to Marine Air Group 13 at Kaneohe Marine Base in Oahu, Hawaii, on the opposite side of the island from Honolulu. He coached and played for the MAG13 football team that consisted of young gunho Marines. "We were well ahead at halftime of the championship playoff game and I learned quickly how rank has its privileges," he said. "Our commanding officer was a major and the opposing team was headed by a colonel. The rules said no additions could be made to the roster during a game. However, at the start of the second half, our opponents had a brand new team."

After the Hawaii experience and military service, he joined Melpar, Inc., an aerospace company in Falls Church, Virginia. With 10 years of experience in manufacturing and contracts he accepted a position with the CIA in Langley. Because of his experience in secret technology development, he was recruited to be vice president of a new company engaged in government intelligence contracts. In 1976 he joined TRW, now Northrop Grumman, in Fairfax, Virginia, where he retired as director of finance after 20 years. He and Shelly now live in Leesburg, Virginia and have a second home in the Northern Neck off the Tappahannock River where they spend time enjoying water activities and fishing with their two daughters, three sons, 10 grandchildren and five great grandchildren.

* Robert E. "Bob" Elzey – Junior, 21, 5'10", 170 – Salisbury, Md. (1932-2002)

Used as a defensive safety man last season only Bob's size holds him out of starting offensive roles. He is a little speedster and can really go in an open field. He was all-State for two years in high school. He is a member of Lambda Chi Alpha fraternity.

Bob spent his career in the U.S. Navy as an aviator and retired in Pensacola, Florida as a Lieutenant Commander. Pensacola, considered the "Cradle of Naval Aviation," is where he took his flight training in 1955. During the Vietnam conflict he had several tours flying AD Skyraiders on numerous combat missions off of an aircraft carrier. Some considered the Douglas Aircraft plane to be the best attack bomber ever built.

In 1968, after serving one season as an assistant coach to former West Virginia running back Bob Moss, he was named head football coach of the Pensacola Naval Air Station Goshawks when Moss was assigned combat duty in Vietnam. With future Hall of Famer Roger Staubach as his quarterback, Bob coached the team to an undefeated season. Many opponents were colleges throughout the Southeast. He retired in 1975 and several years later became head football coach at Pensacola Catholic High School where he also taught math. For more than a decade he was a simulator instructor at Burnside Ott and trained student naval aviators at Ford Aerospace and Loral Aerospace. He had a daughter and a son and three grandchildren.

Aubrey Fitzgerald – Sophomore, 20, 6'0", 190 – Waynesboro, Va. (1953-   )

Held back last season with an elbow injury, the carrot-topped "Fitz" still lacks in experience but makes up for it in his stature and desire to play. He is majoring in physical education and plans to coach in the future.

Aubrey came to W&M planning to be a high school teacher and coach and Howard Smith, professor of kinesiology, was his mentor. His career took a turn when attended an Upjohn Company job fair do a favor for the college's director of placement. The pharmaceutical company offered him a job and he was with Upjohn for 38 years and based the entire time in Newport News. He retired in 1994 as a senior salesman.

He has freely given of his time to public service and was instrumental in the development of both the Oyster Point Business Park and Newport News/Williamsburg International

Airport, which he serves as chairman of the airport commission. He also served on the Newport News City Council for 18 years and two terms as vice mayor. From 1996-2002 he was on the board of directors of the W&M Alumni Association and also served on the board of the Athletic Educational Foundation. He has attended every homecoming since 1952. In 2003 he was awarded the Alumni Medallion, the highest award the W&M Alumni Association can bestow on a graduate of the college. He is married to the former Shirley Richardson ('57) and they have a son, two daughters and five grandchildren.

* Al Grieco – Sophomore, 20, 5'8", 160 – Newark, N.J. (1933-2007)

The diminutive sophomore from Newark schooled and prepped at the same schools as burley tackle George Parozzo – Barringer High School And St. Benedict's Prep. Highly wanted and regarded, he was all-State and all-Metropolitan prior to coming to the Reservation. He was used a lot in defensive roles last season and only his size kept him out of offensive roles. He is the best passer on the team and runs similar to Ed Mioduszewski. Small but shifty, he'll break away plenty before graduation time. A mathematics major, he is a member of Sigma Nu fraternity.

Like many others on the 1953 football team, Grieco was an avid bridge player. For three years he was the starting shortstop on the W&M baseball team. His senior year he was president of Sigma Nu fraternity. After graduation he was commissioned as an officer in the U.S. Army and played football for the Ft. Monmouth team that played other military service teams on the East Coast. Following his active duty military service, he had a successful career in the insurance industry. He retired in 1997 as vice president of claims for the Jefferson Insurance Co. in Jersey City, New Jersey. Previously he had been with the Fireman's Fund Insurance Co. in Newark for many years.

He continued his love of football and early in his career coached high school football. He became a football official and worked high school games into his sixties. He was honored for his athletic achievements at Barringer High School when he was inducted into the Newark (New Jersey) Sports Hall of Fame. He and his wife Grace lived in Bloomfield for 27 years before moving to Verona in 2004 and had two sons and five grandchildren.

* Doug Henley – Sophomore, 19, 6'0", 187 – South Norfolk, Va. (1934-1990)

The stocky red-head probably won't see too much action this year behind Bill Bowman, but displayed tremendous running ability as a freshman. He was awarded the trophy for the most outstanding football player in high school for his section. He'll be one to watch in a couple of years. He is a member of Kappa Alpha fraternity.

After graduation, he married classmate Barbara Ann Pharo ('57) and served in the U.S. Army Reserves, rising to the rank of 1st Lieutenant. He then began his professional career with Texaco, before moving into the commercial building industry. At the time of his death in 1990, he served as director of business development with Meredith Construction in Newport News, Virginia.

Doug availed himself to the benefit of many young athletes. As well as coaching and mentoring football and baseball players, he established an anonymous "Angel Fund" that provided athletic equipment to those that otherwise could afford none. Later, he was a high school football referee in the states of North Carolina, Georgia, and Virginia. He also was very active in the Episcopal Church. Aside from teaching Sunday school, he was a Vestryman and very involved in Cursillo. He embodied the grace of the Holy Spirit and lived accordingly. He and his wife have three children and six grandchildren who reside primarily in Virginia and North Carolina.

* Walter "Shorty" Herrmann – Junior, 24, 5'10", 170 – Warwick, Va. (1929-1994)

A transplanted Georgian, "Shorty" was a starter in the defensive backfield last season and needs to add experience to his running ability. Highly regarded in Savannah where he schooled prior to W&M, he was all-State for two years. He served in the U.S. Air Force from 1950-52. A business administration major he is a member of Kappa Sigma fraternity.

He was an outstanding and highly recruited running back at Savannah High School and his dream was to play at Georgia Tech. After his freshman year in 1948, Coach Bobby Dodd told him he was "too small" to have a scholarship. In 1949 when his parents moved back to Warwick, Virginia, where he was born, he transferred to W&M but was ineligible to compete the first year. When friends in Savannah in the Air Force National Guard were activated to serve in Korea, Shorty enlisted and was stationed at Misawa Air Base in Northern Honshu, Japan. He was a crew chief for fighter planes and played for the Misawa 49ers base football team.

After graduation in 1955 he married Tish Rustad ('55) and joined IBM as a sales trainee in Washington, D.C., and they lived in Shelly Bailey Cox's parent's house in Arlington, Virginia. A year later he was based in Norfolk as a systems engineer. In 1959 he changed to Federal Sales. In 1967 IBM moved him to Fayetteville, N.C. so he could service various military bases in the area. Shorty remained in sales for several years and then moved back to systems. After he retired from IBM in 1986 he continued working with some of his customers. He was a church deacon and Sunday school teacher. He played softball for the church team until he injured his knee in 1984, but continued playing golf and cards. He and Tish have four sons, including twins.

* L. Quinby Hines – Senior, 21, 5'8", 125, Suffolk, Va. (1931-1994)

Starting out as a water boy for the Tribe, he has developed into a dependable extra point man. Nicknamed everything from "Buck" to "Hadacol," L.Q. is the third generation of his family to don the tri-colors of W&M. He ranked 7th in the nation last year with 30-34 PATs (88.2%). Ranking 8th in 1951, he was instrumental in three Indian victories. He is a business administration major and chaplain for Sigma Alpha Epsilon fraternity.

With the encouragement of his father, Lloyd Quinby Hines, Sr., Lloyd Quinby "Hadacol" Hines, Jr. became a place kicker in high school and then followed his father's footsteps playing football at W&M, majoring in business administration and being a member of SAE fraternity. "Horse" Hines' 1926 team posted a 7-3 record losing to Syracuse, Harvard and Columbia with wins over Randolph-Macon, George Washington, Wake Forest and Richmond.

After graduation Quinby was commissioned at Fort Sill, Oklahoma and assigned to Germany. After his military service he returned to Suffolk and joined his father at Ferguson Manufacturing Co., makers of farm equipment and implements. He was active in the Rotary Club, Chamber of Commerce and on the board of the Salvation Army. He served on the board of Main Street Methodist Church and was superintendent of Sunday school for many years. He was president of the W&M Athletic Educational Foundation and loved to fish and duck hunt with his sons. He married the former Ann Cambridge Callihan ('55) and they have two sons and two daughters and seven grandchildren.

* George Karschner – Sophomore, 18, 6'0", 200 – Williamsport, Penn. (1935-1991)

Jack Freeman was his high school coach and recruited him to W&M. On the track team he throws the shot put, discus and javelin.

He withdrew from W&M in March 1955 and died in 1991. No other information is available.

William "Bill" Marfizo – Sophomore, 18, 6'2", 194 – Windber, Penn. (1935-   )

A three-letterman and president of his class in high school, Bill proved himself last season as a linebacker for the Jayvees. Because of the shortage in top flight ends this season, he may also see action at that position. He is a business administration major and a member of Sigma Nu fraternity.

Sportswriters named him "Mr. Versatility" after he played six different positions in the Navy game – his usual center and linebacker positions as well as offensive and defensive end, offensive tackle and defensive halfback. In spite of injuries, he played every game during the season. The following season he blocked a punt in the end zone to give W&M a 2-0 win over Richmond. He was named honorable mention on the Associated Press all-State (Virginia) team. In 1955 he was elected team co-captain with Al Grieco.

After graduation he served six years in the U.S. Army as an artillery officer rising to the rank of captain. Following military service he went to graduate school and received his Doctor of Dental Medicine degree from Temple University and ranked third in a class of 150. Bill was honored with the Arthur Gage Award for having the highest grades during senior exams. He established his dentistry practice in Harrisburg, Pennsylvania and later Camp Hill, a Philadelphia suburb, and has been named to a number of dental and medical honor societies in oral surgery, internal medicine and clinical pathology.

At W&M he was president of the Varsity Club, recipient of the Algernon Sydney Sullivan Humanitarian Award, president of Old Dominion Hall, a distinguished military student and member of Scabbard and Blade. He and his wife Angela live in Mechanicsburg, Pennsylvania and he has three daughters.

William "Bill" Martin – Sophomore, 23, 5'10", 180 – Linden, N.J. (1930-   )

Another dangerous break-away runner is "Wiz" who is a sprinter in track. He was all-State at Linden (N.J.) High School and then played for Hinds (Mississippi) Junior College and Parris Island, when the team won the all-Marine Championship in 1951. Ineligible last season, coaches believed that Bill could have broken into the "Lonesome Foursome" backfield. Majoring in physical education he hopes to teach and coach after graduation. He is a member of Sigma Nu fraternity.

A Korean veteran, he was went to Hines Junior College where he was recruited by Rube McCray and had to sit out the 1952 season as a transfer. Being a veteran he had a car and would drive Al Grieco and George Parozzo to and from campus when they were all students and fraternity brothers. After graduating in 1955 he returned home to Linden and taught and coached at his high school for 36 years. He lives in Bayville, N.J. and has three sons and two grandchildren.

The first seven years at Linden High School, Bill taught classes and was the freshman coach in football, basketball and baseball. Then he became the head coach of football and track and later took over the high school's golf team. His last five years he also was the assistant athletic director. He was involved in civic and community groups in Linden and coached little league teams as his sons were growing up. When he retired he began swimming at the local YMCA and playing golf. In 2009, after three years of dialysis, he had a kidney transplant thanks to his son. "I love to tell everyone that I may be 81 years old but I have a 41-year-old kidney," Bill says.

* Grover T. "Tommy" Martin – Senior, 24, 5'11", 205 – Roanoke, Va. (1929-2010)

Co-captain along with Steve Milkovich, Martin is perhaps the most versatile member of the squad. "Red Dog" played blocking back in the old single wing and last season switched to tackle when a leg injury he suffered with the U.S. Marine Corps in combat in Korea slowed him down. Feeling he's worked it out he can really move as a halfback – all 205 pounds of him. He was all-everything in high school for Jefferson Senior and also played one year with the Camp Lejune Marines. Married, he is majoring in physical education and is undecided between the F.B.I. and coaching as a career. A Dean's List student, he is a member of Sigma Alpha Epsilon fraternity.

He was honorable mention all-State (Virginia) by AP and a pre-season Academic all-American. His W&M years were interrupted when he served with the U.S. Marines in Korea and was awarded the Purple Heart for battle wounds. He also ran track and played baseball for W&M. As a student he was in Alpha Kappa Delta sociology honorary fraternity, the Varsity Club and the Spanish Club. He joined the FBI in 1954 and served for 26 years as a special agent with distinction. His assignments were in New York City; Pittsburgh; Beckley, W.Va.; and Richmond and Radford, Va.. Following retirement, for five years he taught at police schools in Latin America and the Caribbean and for 15 years was a field representative for the Motion Picture Association of America.

Tommy held longtime memberships in the Order of the Purple Heart, the Order of White Jacket, Fraternal Order of Police, National Association of Retired Federal Employees, Virginia Heights Masonic Lodge, Scottish Rites Bodies and the Kazim Temple. He was an active member of Grove United Methodist Church for 35 years. He and Katherine Bell Martin ('51) lived in Radford and they have two sons, a daughter and two grand children.

Steve Milkovich – Junior, 22, 5"11", 195 – Johnstown, Penn. (1931-   )

"Weed" as he is tabbed by his friends comes from one of Pennsylvania's foremost football towns. Elected as a co-captain of the 1953 football team, Steve may be held back from a starting position by his lack of speed. Last season he was primarily a defensive guard and made the Big Green line impenetrable. He needs to add speed to his offensive play. In high school he was picked as "Lineman of the Year" at the same time that Tommy Yewcic of Michigan State and younger brother of W&M's former Paul, was picked as "Back of the Year." A business administration major, he plans to be an accountant. He is treasurer of his fraternity, Lambda Chi Alpha, as well as the Inter-Fraternity Council.

Instead of ROTC, Steve was in the Marine Platoon Leaders Class but after four months on active duty was given a medical discharge because of traumatic arthritic damages to both of his knees. Because he did not have two years of active military service, he was then drafted in the U.S. Army but after nine months released because of his knees. He took a job with the Internal Revenue Service and was a field auditor for two years.

In 1957 he then moved to Oberlin, Ohio, his home today, and bought a dry cleaning and laundry business that he owned and operated for 52 years. During this same period for 37 years he owned two coin-operated laundries and nine commercial buildings. He married Donna Henninger of Lorain, Ohio in 1959 and they have three children, nine grand children and one great grand child.

* Bill Nagy – Sophomore, 20, 5'11", 180 – Baker Whitely, Penn. (1933-1973)

Outstanding in high school as a scholar, leader, and athlete, "Nagaski" will have to overcome an injured knee to be able to see much action this season. Showed much promise as a frosh last year on the Jayvees. He is a member of Sigma Nu fraternity and plans to major in physical education and then coach.

He competed against teammate Bill Riley in high school and the two became roommates at W&M. After graduation in 1956, he became a science teacher and coach at Oscar Smith High School in South Norfolk, Virginia in the Chesapeake Public Schools system. In June 1967 he transferred to the Virginia Beach Schools district and taught science at

Floyd E. Kellam High School. In 1969 he moved to Plaza Junior High School as a science teacher. He and his family were killed in a tragic automobile accident near Fredericksburg, Virginia on May 13, 1973 while on vacation.

*** George Parozzo – Senior, 22, 6"2", 235 – Newark, N.J. (1931-2002)**

Is like a bear in the Indians forward wall. He has been used primarily on defense but will have no trouble at all adapting himself for offensive duty. Attended Barringer High School and prepped at St. Benedict's Prep in New Jersey. For his aggressiveness in the Big Green's 20-14 victory over Penn in 1951, he was named to the United Press all-America team (honorable mention). Is plenty fast for his size and has exceptional strength. He is another one of William & Mary's many candidates for the professional ranks. An economic major, he is a member of Sigma Nu fraternity.

He was named to the first team all-Southern Conference and first team all-State (Virginia) by both AP and UPI. He was the fifth choice in the NFL draft by Detroit and played briefly with the Lions before joining the Hamilton (Ontario) Tiger Cats in the Canadian Football League. He was forced to retire because of his knees. George, whose father was the Chief Deputy U.S. Marshal for New Jersey, was an outstanding high school athlete in both basketball and football. After playing football professionally, he returned to St. Benedict's Prep as a coach for five years. Then for 33 years, he taught grades five to eight at elementary schools in Newark's inner-city. He had a love and passion for history and geography, his favorite subjects, as well as Greek and Latin. At W&M he took classes in Greek every year and some semesters as well as Latin.

When a group of cousins made a trip to a Connecticut casino, he dominated the conversation all the way there explaining historical details about the Tappan Zee Bridge, Story of Sleepy Hollow, the headless horseman, Rip Van Winkle and the life of Washington Irving. When a cousin told him that he hadn't stopped talking, George responded "That's right. And I'm gonna ask questions on the way back!"

His cousin describes him as the kindest, sweetest, most sensitive person she ever met. He loved food and on holidays would count out his mother's ravioli and yell "Make 50 more, Ma!" He also loved to tell jokes and continued his love of sports by talking back to the television commentators when he disagreed with a call. He and his wife, Rosa, lived in North Arlington.

*** Jack Place – Senior, 23, 5'11", 175 – Spencerville, Ohio (1929-1997)**

Diminutive but swift, Jack fitted well into the defensive backfield plans of Jack Freeman last season. While in the U.S. Marine Corps he played with teams at Quantico and also with Tommy Martin and Harry Agganis at Camp Lejune. Married, he is a Dean's List student and majoring in accounting. He hopes to join the F.B.I. upon graduation. Also a member of the accounting club and the varsity club, he is president of his fraternity, Phi Kappa Tau.

He was a pre-season Academic all-American and graduated Phi Beta Kappa with a degree in business administration. He continued on at W&M to receive his bachelor of civil law and master's of law and taxation degrees. For years he practiced law in Roanoke and was a director of the Roanoke Bar Association. He was a partner in the law firm of Apostolou, Place, Thomas & Prillman and later senior partner in the firm of Jolly, Place, Falin and Prillman, P.C.

Jack was a member of the America Bar Association, Roanoke Moose Lodge, president of the W&M Roanoke Alumni Chapter, and served as Western Virginia Trustee for the W&M Athletic Education Foundation. He retired as a Lt. Colonel in the Marine Corps Reserves. At W&M he lettered in football for four years, ran track, and was a member of Phi Alpha Delta law fraternity. He also was elected to Phi Beta Kappa and Omicron Delta Kappa honorary fraternities. He had three children and three grandchildren.

William "Bill" Riley – Sophomore, 19, 5'11", 160 – Holsopple, Penn. (1934-   )

The stocky red-head should come around with more experience. He must add weight to his frame before he can be expected to take all the knocks of the game.

Like many other W&M athletes, Bill grew up in a small coal mining town in the Johnstown, Pennsylvania area. In high school he competed against future teammates Bill Nagy and Bill Marfizo, also Iron Indians, as well as Jim Kaplan of Kaplan Arena fame. He and Nagy were roommates for two years. Bill entered the U.S. Army in 1957 and after basic training was assigned to Ft. Bliss, Texas, where he taught basic electronics for the M33 radar system. In 1959 he was hired by the National Academy of Sciences in Washington, D.C. as an accountant and became responsible for more than 2,000 contracts. NAS sent him to school for data processing and he later designed a new payroll system and other accounting programs and systems for the institution.

After 13 years at NAS, he and a friend and NAS colleague decided to go into business for themselves in the Frederick, Maryland area. They purchased one service station in 1973, and their entrepreneurial success expanded to owning three service stations, an ice cream store, laundromats, produce markets and rental income properties. He married his wife Paulette in August 1962 and they have a son, a daughter and three grandsons. His daughter completed advanced degrees at Delaware and George Washington and worked at Johns Hopkins Medical Center until home schooling her three sons. Bill's son graduated from South Carolina, was a competitor in both mountain biking and eco challenges around the world and is a senior analyst for Booz Allen Hamilton. Following in the footsteps of their grandfather, his three grandsons are all active in sports.

John Risjord – Junior, 20, 6'2", 170 – Kansas City, Missouri (1933-   )

Experience will be a big drawback for this lanky speed merchant who is trying his first hand at football. Outstanding in track, he excels in the high jump, broad jump and low hurdles. He is a business administration major and a member of Pi Kappa Alpha fraternity.

Another Dean's List student, after graduation in 1954, he earned his law degree at the University of Wisconsin. He practiced trial law for 40 years in Kansas City and was admitted to practice in Missouri, Kansas, and Colorado, the 8th, 9th, and 10th Circuits of the U.S. Courts of Appeals and the U.S. Supreme Court. He was appointed legal counsel by the Judicial Panel of the U.S. to handle consolidated cases from across the country involving explosive separation of multi-piece truck wheels and handled the trial of some of those cases in state and federal courts in 26 states and the District of Columbia.

He tried product liability cases all across the U.S. and twice argued before the U.S. Supreme Court, once as a defendant, Firestone v. Risjord. Mike Wallace did a documentary on the case for *60 Minutes*, "Killer Wheels," for which Wallace and CBS won an Emmy from the Academy of Television Arts & Sciences. He and his wife Sally, a graduate of Kansas State, have two sons, a daughter and two grandchildren. They split their time between homes in Snowman Village, Colorado and Koloa, Kaua'i Hawai'i.

Jerry Sazio – Junior, 20, 6'0", 220 – Irvington, N.J. (1933-   )

"Jarring Jerry" is his appropriate nickname and exactly what he does every Saturday afternoon to opposing backs. He's one man to avoid and keep out of the way of on a gridiron, but after the final gun sounds, he's docile as a lamb. Inactive last season, during his sophomore year in 1951 he earned the reputation as one of the outstanding linebackers in this section of the country. He is perhaps the strongest man in a football uniform in the South today. He will be a sure bet for all-star balloting this fall. Is a younger bother of Ralph, who co-captained the 1947 Southern Conference Champions Indians. Has picked up 20 pounds and is like a mad charging bull. He is a member of Sigma Nu fraternity and a business administration major.

In January he was elected co-captain for the '54 season along with Charlie Sumner, following in the footsteps of his older brother Ralph. His senior year, Jerry was named first team all-Southern Conference beating out West Virginia University's Sam Huff, a consensus all-American who later was inducted in the Pro Football Hall of Fame. In 1951 he also was named all-Southern Conference. In 1955 he was drafted by the Chicago (now Phoenix) Cardinals of the National Football League but chose to play for the Hamilton Tiger Cats in the Canadian league. He was given a $500 signing bonus by head coach Carl Voyles, who coached W&M to a 29-7-3 record from 1939-1942, and his brother Ralph was an assistant coach at Hamilton.

Off-season he worked for the AAA in Norfolk until he took a job as assistant football coach at Maury High School and taught physical education in elementary and middle schools. In 1963 he became Maury's head football coach and after his first season, for the next 12 years, he never had a losing season. His 1972 team was runner-up for the Virginia state championship. In 1975 he became Maury's athletic director at Maury until retiring in 1997.

In 2006 his former players endowed the Jerry Sazio Football Scholarship at Maury. A fund raiser golf tournament is held every May that now provides four students with

$1,000 each year for four years of college. His wife, the former Dorothy Bailey ('53) was a counselor at Maury. They have two daughters and a son and five grandchildren and live in Virginia Beach. In 2006 he was inducted in the Columbia High School Hall of Fame in South Orange, N.J. In 2000 he was elected to the W&M Sports Hall of Fame for individual honors and in 1979 was inducted as part of the Iron Indians team.

* Sam Scott – Junior, 21, 6"2", 200 – Hopewell, Virginia (1931-1991)

Sam has held down an offensive tackle post and has been a letterman for his two years here at the Reservation. He played center for Hopewell in high school and was all-State. He doesn't have a care in the world off the gridiron, but really means business every Saturday during the season. He has constantly developed and picked up needed experience the past two years and will be great to look for. He is a member of Kappa Sigma fraternity.

In 1954 Sam married Lollie Egger ('55), a cheerleader and "Miss William & Mary of 1954." The couple graduated in 1955 following the birth of their first son, Lester. Sam enlisted in the U.S. Army and was based at Ft. Sill, Oklahoma. After three years and with three sons, he returned to civilian life and accepted a job in St. Petersburg, Florida with Florida Power Corporation, now Florida Progress.

He was promoted to district director and relocated to Monticello, Florida where he was active in the company as well as community, civic and church organizations until his death. He was a long time member of the Sertoma service club and was governor of all of the chapters in Florida. Well respected in the Monticello area, he also served on the vestry of his Episcopal church. Lollie earned her master's degree in social work at Florida State University. They have two grandchildren.

Charlie Sumner – Junior, 22, 6'1", 185 – Salem, Va. (1930-   )

The expected return of the lanky speedster will greatly strengthen the Indian backfield. A good passer and deceptive runner, he will be remembered for his 89-yard kickoff return in W&M's 20-14 victory over Penn in 1951. Was used primarily as a defensive safety man and understudy of Dickie Lewis on offense in 1951.

He was named first team all-State (Virginia) by both AP and UPI. His 89-yard second half kickoff return in W&M's 20-14 win over Penn in 1951 is still a Franklin Field record. He was elected co-captain of the 1954 team along with Jerry Sazio. While only a junior, he was drafted by the Chicago Bears. In 1955 he became the starting safety for the Bears. He broke his jaw in the last pre-season game, it was wired, he played half the season that way, and was named the Bears' Rookie of the Year. His NFL career was interrupted for two years when he served in the U.S. Army. He returned to the Bears in 1958 and played three more seasons for the Bears. For the Bears he also returned 11 kickoffs for 307 yards including an 81-yard touchdown run. Then he was drafted for the new expansion Minnesota Vikings where he played two seasons before becoming a coach. Charlie led the Vikings in tackles and played the entire last season with a broken wrist. During his nine-season NFL career he intercepted 21 passes and once recovered a fumble that he ran back 86 yards for a touchdown.

In 1963 he joined the Oakland Raiders as an assistant coach and soon would be considered the number one defensive coordinator in professional football. In 1968 the Raiders won the AFL and lost 33-14 to the Green Bay Packers which had won the first Super Bowl played the year before. A year later he joined the Pittsburgh Steelers and helped build their dynasty before moving to the New England Patriots in 1973. The Raiders brought him back in 1979 and Oakland won Super Bowl XV beating the Philadelphia Eagles 27-10. Sumner's 1983 defensive team was considered one of the most ferocious to play in the NFL. *Sports Illustrated* credited Sumner's defensive strategy for beating the Washington Redskins 38-9 to win Super Bowl XVIII. In 1985 he was head coach of the Oakland Invaders of the USFL which lost the championship game 28-24 to the Baltimore Stars. He then retired from professional football and moved to Maui so he could play golf every day.

Charlie has coached a number of players who have been inducted in the NFL Pro Football Hall of Fame including Howie Long, Willie Brown, Gene Upshaw, Art Shell, Ted Hendricks and Mike Haynes. All say it would not have been possible without the way they were coached by him. In 2007 he was inducted in the Virginia Sports Hall of Fame. He has two sons and lives with June Raymond in Lahaina, Maui, Hawai'i.

* Chet Waksmunski – Sophomore, 18, 6"1", 197 – Hastings, Penn. (1935-2003)

Only 18, his stocky physique hardly reveals his near 200 pounds. Has exceptional speed for his size and can easily fit into the one-platoon system with his all-around ability. A mathematics major, he is a member of Sigma Nu fraternity.

He came to W&M from the small coal mining town of Hastings, near Johnstown and 70 miles east of Pittsburgh. The population in 2000 was 1,398, smaller than the W&M student body. After graduation in 1956 he went to work for Westinghouse Electric Corporation for a year before serving as an officer in the U.S. Army for two years. He returned to Westinghouse in 1959 and worked in Baltimore on radar systems.

After 38 years he retired as a manager of engineering operations for Westinghouse. During this time he always found time to be active in civic and charitable organizations, coached little league football and basketball, coached at St. Johns Catholic School and served as president of the Kiwanis. After retirement he spent time fishing and crabbing in the Chesapeake Bay. He met his wife Linda at Westinghouse and they lived in Severna Park, Maryland, have four children and seven grandchildren.

The Coaches and Staff

The following profiles of the coaches and staff of the 1953 William & Mary Iron Indians are reprinted from the 1953 W&M football media guide. Following the publication (in boldface italics) is a summary of their professional careers.

* Deceased

* John J. "Jackie" Freeman (W&M 1947) – Head Coach (1918-2003)

Returning as head football coach for the second successive season is former W&M grid star, John Joseph "Jackie" Freeman. A member of the 1941, 1942 and 1946 teams, he came to W&M in 1940 after spending a year at the University of Notre Dame and despite his lack of size, blossomed into just the spark that was needed to give the vaunted Tribe juggernaut its impetus to roll over its opposition from Saturday to Saturday.

From his post at tailback, it was the tiny Freeman, then a dynamite of 155 pounds, who paced the 1942 Braves to a great season and the Southern Conference championship. The Windber, Pennsylvania native added basketball and track laurels to his football achievements and was one of the most popular young men on campus.

Then in 1943, he answered the call to service to enter the U.S. Navy. After completing his training he was commissioned an officer and served with distinction aboard an amphibious cargo ship, taking part in many Pacific operations. After his discharge he returned to Williamsburg in 1946.

Having one year of eligibility remaining, Jack traded his officer's blues for the Tribe's tri-colors of Green, Gold and Silver and got back in harness at tailback for Coach Rube McCray's squad, which captured eight wins in 10 games, losing only to Miami and "Choo Choo" Justice-favored North Carolina.

The next June, Freeman was awarded his B.S. in physical education. It was the beginning of his career as a coach. His native Pennsylvania, perhaps the most noted of all football incubators, was quick to grab him up. Coaching posts at McKeesport and Williamsport served as his orientation in the art of handling young athletes.

Jack's return to W&M after his Navy duty was also the occasion for him to meet co-ed Jane Achenbach, who also received her degree in 1947. The Freeman's have two daughters, Susan and Patty.

The T-formation came to W&M in 1951 when Marvin Bass took over the reins following the resignation of McCray. Bass, one of the nation's most promising young coaches, recognized Freeman's abilities and football knowledge and beckoned him to the Reservation as backfield coach. Another great year resulted for the Indians with seven victories including wins over Penn, Duke, Wake Forest and Boston University.

The departure of Bass to the professional Washington Redskins left things in a state of flux at W&M. However, a few weeks later and after an interim appointment of alumnus J. M. Eason, President Alvin Duke Chandler solidified matters with the announcement that the Tribe's new coach would be Freeman.

On the 10th anniversary of William & Mary's first Southern Conference championship, the 1942 tailback Freeman became the 1952 Coach Freeman. His appointment to the football helm also saw him elevated to the post of Athletic Director.

Although comparatively young as coaches go, he has the maturity necessary for the job. At 34 he has spent more than half of his life learning the basics of athletic competition. Four years as an officer in the U.S. Navy helped teach him the value and necessity of order and discipline. His personality, congenial relationship with the men on his staff and the boys on his squad, make him an ideal person for the task at hand.

As a player he was described as "a superb punter and a tricky runner, and the little jack rabbit is a keen student of the game." As a coach, although his full success cannot yet be measured, he could be called "a great handler of men, popular with his players and staff, and still a keen student of the game.

Last season under Freeman the Indians compiled a 4-5 record which could be termed a credible performance considering the caliber of opposition. This season, the first for the "new" Southern Conference, the situation doesn't look overly promising, but the Tribe could surprise. In any case, don't underestimate the coach talent of Head Coach Jack Freeman.

With the success of the Iron Indians Jack Freeman was named the Big Six Coach of the Year. Few college coaches have ever achieved what he did with the Iron Indians that season – a winning season playing a major schedule with only 24 players and 15 scholarships. Today teams have 120 players on a team and the NCAA allows 85 scholarships. In spite of the success of the 1953 season, the college's commitment to football continued to steadily decline. When he finished the fifth year of his contract, he was offered a one-year extension, but with no money for scholarships to recruit student athletes, he resigned on July 1, 1957 to accept a management job with the Great Atlantic & Pacific Tea Company, better known as A&P. During his tenure the W&M football budget was decreased by $40,000 to only $31,434 – compared, for example, to $81,379 at VPI – and coaches from a staff of six to only three. His overall record coaching W&M teams from 1952 through 1956 was 14-29-3.

As a student he lettered in football, basketball and track. Only 5'6", he was the tailback on the 1941 team that had an 8-2 record and the 1942 team that won the Southern Conference Championship, had a 9-1-1 record and lost only to a star-studded North Carolina Pre-Flight team of future aviators. The team beat Oklahoma in post-season play. After the season he enlisted in the U.S. Navy and was placed in the prestigious V-12 program with officer training at the University of Richmond. Jack and W&M teammates Lou Hoitsma and Marvin Bass, also in the program, led Richmond to one of its best seasons ever in 1943 losing only once in seven games, to Duke, which also had a V-12 team of college stars. At both W&M and Richmond he was named to the All-Virginia and All-Southern teams. For the first time in 50 years W&M did not field a football team in 1943 otherwise he and other Indians would have to play against their alma mater.

Jack was commissioned after eight months of training and served with distinction in the South Pacific with actions including Okinawa. He then served in the occupations of Korea and China before he returned to W&M at tailback for a 1946 team that had an 8-2 record, losing only to Miami and North Carolina.

He and Jane Achenbach were married after the two graduated in 1947. He became the high school coach at McKeesport, Pennsylvania, some 80 miles from his hometown of Windber, where he quarterbacked the 1936 high school team to an undefeated season that earned him a scholarship at Notre Dame. After two successful seasons he moved to Williamsport High School until he was recruited by Marvin Bass to be the W&M assistant backfield coach.

He was with A&P for 21 years with senior positions in Richmond, Baltimore and Raleigh, N.C. His love of coaching kept him involved with little league teams. In 1979, Bob Thalman, the head coach at VMI, lured Jack back to college football to coach the offensive backs. Thalman, who succeeded W&M's Vito Ragazzo at VMI in 1970, had awarded Freeman's son Mike a football scholarship to play on the 1975-1977 teams.

Jack and Jane were residents of Lexington, Virginia in 1984, when Thalman retired. Next-door-neighbor Washington & Lee recruited Jack to coach the offensive backs for the Generals. He agreed only if he did not have to travel with the team.

Two years later, he thought he had retired and was enjoying playing golf when the local high school in Lexington, where Jane happened to teach math, called for his help. The day before football practice was to begin the coach was offered a college coaching job and accepted it. The school had five different coaches in five years. He agreed to coach the team for one year and at age 67 became one of the oldest high school football coaches in the country. He has been inducted in the W&M Sports Hall of Fame. Jack and Jane have three daughters, two sons and nine grandchildren.

Eric Tipton (Duke 1939) – Assistant Coach (1915-2001)

The senior member of the coaching staff is tremendously popular Eric Tipton, a native of Petersburg, Virginia, and former all-time great athlete at Duke. "Tip" has been on the staff at W&M since his graduation and last spring accepted the position of baseball coach after turning down several professional managerial positions. A former major league baseball player with Cincinnati and Philadelphia, and top batter with the Portland Beavers in 1952, he returns for his 14th season with the Tribe.

He came first to mold the pre-war squads of Carl Voyles, then assisted Rube McCray, stayed on with Marvin Bass, and now is aiding Jack Freeman. He is now almost a legend with Southern sports writers and radio announcers. Married to a former W&M co-ed, he makes his home in Williamsburg all year-round. He has four children, three girls and one boy.

Eric "The Red" Tipton was one of the greatest athletes to come out of Petersburg, Virginia. In 1965 he was inducted into the College Football Hall of Fame. He also has been inducted in the Virginia, W&M and Duke Sports Halls of Fame. One of his most remarkable feats was in Duke's 7-0 over Pittsburgh in the Rose Bowl in 1938 when he kicked seven punts inside Pitt's 10-yard line and another seven within the 20-yard line. His punting average was 41.3 yards with a return average of only 1.2.

He was co-captain of the 1938 team that was considered the greatest in Duke history. Called the Iron Dukes, it won all nine of its regular season games without ever being scored on. The team lost its final game in the 1939 Rose Bowl as Southern California scored in the last minute of the game to win 7-3. He was drafted by the Washington Redskins but chose to play professional baseball with the Philadelphia Athletics and Toronto in the AAA International League. From 1942-1945 he played for the Cincinnati Reds until he was sold in 1946 to the St. Paul Saints of the American Association. In 1952 he moved to Portland, Oregon where he played for one season before retiring.

He joined the W&M coaching staff a few months after graduating from Duke in 1939 and took responsibility as backfield coach. From 1953-1957 he also was head baseball coach. After 18 years at W&M, in 1957 he moved to the U.S. Military Academy at West Point as head coach of the baseball and lightweight football teams. He compiled a record 234-201-5 and five league titles in baseball and the Cadet's 150-pound football team had a 104-14-1 record, .878 winning percentage, and 13 league championships. He retired in 1977 and returned to his home in Williamsburg. He and his wife Gertrude had four children and nine grandchildren.

* Herbert "Neepie" Miller (Washington & Lee 1950) – Assistant Coach (1922-1998)

A former football star with Washington & Lee, easy-going Herb Miller received his first coaching assignment as freshman coach at his alma mater under George Barclay in 1950. He now begins his third year with the Indians as line coach. He boasts a large fund of basic football knowledge and commands both respect and popularity from the boys on the squad as well as the other students on the Reservation.

At Petersburg High School he played football, ran track and wrestled. He enrolled at W&M in 1942 but left the following year to join the U.S. Navy. After his discharge in 1946 as a Chief Petty Officer, he was lured to transfer to Washington & Lee by Art "Pappy" Lewis, the Generals' head coach before he moved to West Virginia University. An injury cut his playing days short and "Neepie" became a student coach and graduated in 1950. He returned to W&M as a line coach for Marvin Bass and join the Indians' staff with another Petersburg legend, Eric Tipton, who was his "best man" at his wedding.

In 1955 he married Dorothy "Dot" Lyons from Petersburg and he left W&M in 1956 to enter private business in Bluefield, W. Va. They have a son, a daughter and two grand children. They returned home in 1963 when he was named coach and physical education instructor at the new Richard Bland College of The College of William & Mary. Using a former dairy barn as a gymnasium, he developed the physical education program to accommodate the growing student body of the junior college. In 1973 he supervised the design and construction of a new facility to house coed sports, fitness and classroom activities. Miller served as head coach for the school's basketball and baseball teams, sponsored sports clinics on the RBC campus, was named Associated Professor of Physical Education and was active until his retirement in 1989.

In addition to his position at RBC, he worked summers as manager of the Battlefield Park Swim Club and supervised many of the city's youths as lifeguards. He also worked many years with the city's Parks and Recreation Department as the supervisor of the two city swimming pools. He still found time to work with kids at the YMCA. A scholarship has been established in his name at Richard Bland to honor his legacy.

* Boydson Baird (Maryville College 1941) – Freshman Coach (1919-2010)

Amiable Boyd starts his second season with W&M and will handle the Tribe Freshman and Junior Varsity. During the winter season, however, he takes over the reins as head basketball coach. He was former head basketball coach for three years at Davidson and is the father of twins – a boy and a girl.

Boyd was head basketball coach and freshman football coach at W&M until returning to his alma mater, Maryville College in Maryville, Tennessee in 1959 as athletic director, head football coach and assistant professor of physical education. In five seasons his Tribe basketball teams compiled a record of 51-73. In six seasons at Maryville his football teams had a 27-23 record and the 1963 team was the best with an 8-1 record. He coached the basketball team for several seasons and is the third-winningest baseball coach in Maryville history. His 1974 baseball team was the first in any Maryville sport to qualify for an NCAA post-season tournament.

Born and raised in Kilbourne, Ohio, Boyd followed his brothers to Maryville where he earned 10 varsity letters in basketball, baseball, football and track. After serving in the

U.S. Army in the Pacific Theatre during World War II, he did graduate work at Ohio Wesleyan and then earned his master's degree in recreational and physical education at Indiana University. The basketball team plays all of its home games in the college's Boydson Baird Gymnasium.

Joseph C. Mark (W&M 1951) – Assistant Coach (1930-   )

He played on the 1947-1950 football teams that compiled a 26-15-2 record. The 1947 team won the Southern Conference Championship and lost to Arkansas 21-19 in the Dixie Bowl. The following year the team went to the Delta Bowl. His senior year he co-captained the team with Vito Ragazzo. He also ran track, was president of the Monogram Club, a member of student assembly and vice president of Sigma Alpha Epsilon fraternity. In 1983 he was inducted in the W&M Sports Hall of Fame.

In 1954 he was assistant coach at Vero Beach (Florida) High School but returned to W&M in 1956 as an assistant. In 1959 he became assistant football coach at North Carolina, turning down an offer in 1963 to return to W&M to succeed Milt Drewer. In 1968 he reunited at the U.S. Naval Academy with two W&M friends, former teammate Jack Cloud and John Cox, sports information director. In 1969 he was an assistant at Maryland for three seasons followed by four at Virginia.

In 1976 Joe became head football coach at Shippensburg University and in three seasons the Red Raiders twice won the Pennsylvania State Athletic Conference Championship. He had a combined record of 21-9-1 before returning to UVa in 1978. Ironically, he was succeeded at Shippensburg by his former teammate, Vito Ragazzo, who was head coach until 1985. At UVa he was involved in fund raising and development for 12 years and served as president of the Virginia Sports Hall of Fame. When basketball coach Terry Holland became athletic director at Davidson, Joe followed him to continue athletic development and also coach golf until retiring in 2000. He and his wife Faith Ann live in Davidson and have a son and a daughter and three grandchildren.

* John L. Clements (North Carolina 1950) – Assistant Coach (1925-1992)

Johnny played wingback in the backfield with Charlie "Choo Choo" Justice during Carolina's greatest football era. He was a four-year letterman, weighed only 165 pounds, played both offense and defense and sometimes was the punter. He was captain of his Crewe, Virginia, high school team. Clements also played baseball for the Tar Heels. After graduation he became a teacher and coach at Whiteville (North Carolina) High School before joining the staff at W&M. After the '53 season he became a sales representative for U.S. Rubber Co. A teacher, coach and athletic administrator, he taught health and physical education at North Carolina State from 1967-1971 and was head coach of the Wolfpack freshman football team. He was instrumental in bringing the Fellowship of Christian Athletes to North Carolina and travelled across the state helping coaches get "huddles" groups started.

For 13 years until his retirement in 1984, Clements was director of health, physical education and recreation for the Wake County Public School system. After retirement he was a financial aid advisor to a high school, counselor of Biblical Wellness Ministries and an instructor for coaches with the Raleigh Parks and Recreation Department. During the 1960s he operated the Johnny Clements Adventure Camp, a day camp for boys and girls ages 6 to 14. In 1977 for five years he was president of the board of directors at Camp Oak Hill in Raleigh. He was an elder emeritus at First Presbyterian Church in Raleigh. He and his wife Mary Louise Rice Clements have two daughters, a son and four grandchildren.

Frank H. "Sonny" Cowling, Sr. (W&M 1953) – Assistant Coach (1931-   )

Sonny played end for four years and was named captain of the defensive team when W&M scrimmaged Maryland. He blocked three punts in one game against an Alex Webster-led North Carolina State. Webster went on to play for the New York Giants and was inducted in the NFL's Pro Football Hall of Fame. Sonny also ran the high and low hurdles in track and won several meets. He came to W&M after playing four years at Newport News High School and one year at the Newport News Shipyard Apprentice School. He was W&M's chief scout during the 1953 season. An economics major, he was vice president of the Varsity Club and a member of Sigma Alpha Epsilon fraternity.

After graduation Sonny was commissioned in the U.S. Army at Ft. Sill, Oklahoma. He then joined the 11th Airborne Division as a paratrooper and made some 30 jumps before he left the 82nd Airborne Division at Ft. Bragg, North Carolina. He returned to Virginia and became an insurance agent and was in that field until retiring. He found time to coach for his former W&M Coach, Rube McCray, at the Apprentice School; campaign in several offshore sailing races; and become singles tennis champion at the James River Country Club where he also plays golf with former teammate Swanson Hornsby. Sonny and his wife Susan live in Hampton, Virginia.

* Guilford Moses "Bill" Joyner (North Carolina 1950) – Trainer (1923-2004)

The man behind the scenes is trainer Bill Joyner whose responsibility is to keep the boys in shape so the Tribe can field a team minus injuries. After coaching cross country, indoor and outdoor track, he teaches several physical education courses. He is a former star high jumper with the Tar Heels. He is married and has one daughter. This will be his second year at the Reservation.

Bill Joyner was a paratrooper in Company D of the 511th Parachute Infantry during World War II. After his active military service in the U.S. Army, he enrolled at North Carolina and graduated with a master's degree in education. He was captain of the track team and broke the collegiate high jump record during a meet in Florida. Following W&M, he was at Dartmouth, where he was named U.S. Athletic Trainer of the Year, and then New Mexico State in Las Cruces. He moved to Albuquerque in 1964 and retired as a teacher from Albuquerque Public Schools. He and his wife Arneta have three daughters, a son, nine grandchildren and a great-grandchild.

* William S. "Pappy" Gooch (Virginia 1918) – Business Manager (1895-1992)

William S. "Pappy" Gooch came to W&M in 1928 to be director of athletics and during his tenure Cary Field was built. He served in that position for the next 11 years until he became the department's business manager. Except for his military service during World War II as Lt. Commander in the U.S. Navy, he handled all business matters for athletics until his retirement in 1964. Because of his love and devotion to W&M, many called him "Mr. William and Mary."

The son of a circuit court judge, he was born in Roanoke and grew up on a family plantation in Louisa County. He graduated from Jefferson School for Boys in Charlottesville and attended Fishburne Military Academy in Waynesboro before entering the University of Virginia. He became one of UVa's greatest athletes quarterbacking the football team to wins over Yale, North Carolina and Vanderbilt. He also starred in basketball, baseball and track.

After graduation he taught and coached at Christchurch School and St. Christopher's School in Richmond and then returned to UVa to serve as an assistant coach. While at W&M he was either a head or assistant coach in football, baseball, track, golf, swimming, boxing and wrestling. During World War I he served in the U.S. Marines. He was inducted in the W&M Sports Hall of Fame in 1971 and in 1965 was honored by UVa with the Thomas Jefferson Award for his embodiment of Jefferson's ideas of education and physical fitness. In 1986 he was inducted in the Virginia Sports Hall of Fame.

Rene A. Henry (W&M '54) – Athletic Press Secretary (1933-   )

Rene entered W&M in February 1951 and worked as an assistant in the sports information office. In February 1953, in the second semester of his junior year, and carrying an 18-hour course load, he was named to that position when Sam Banks joined the Baltimore Colts. At the same time he also was a student assistant in intramural athletics to Dudley Jensen and an officer of Sigma Nu fraternity.

After graduation he became sports information director at West Virginia University from 1954-1956. The next two years when he was on active military duty he was assigned to the athletic department at the U.S. Military Academy at West Point. His work in sports and public relations continued throughout his career and on a worldwide basis. In 1975 in he co-founded what became the second largest public relations firm in the U.S. and the first to establish divisions in sports marketing and Hispanic marketing. The firm was headquartered in Los Angeles with offices in New York, Washington, D.C. and Paris. As a volunteer he directed the global media campaign to bring the 1984 Olympic Games to Los Angeles and served the U.S. Olympic Committee in various capacities for several years. He also was president and CEO of the National Institute of Building Sciences; in 1988 organized the athletes and entertainers for the presidential campaign to elect George H.W. Bush; and later served in federal service positions at the U.S. Department of Labor and Environmental Protection Agency.

His diverse career includes senior positions in housing and real estate, television and motion pictures, and higher education. He has authored seven books and co-written two screenplays. Among numerous honors and awards, the Public Relations Society of America honored him with its Lund Award for Public Service and three Silver Anvils for outstanding excellence in campaigns. In 2001 he was inducted into the Granby High School (Norfolk, Virginia) Hall of Fame. Whenever he has been asked, he has always helped W&M. In 2004 he was awarded the W&M Alumni Association's service award and in 2011 the Alumni Medallion. He now lives in Seattle, has a son, a daughter and a granddaughter.

The Season

W&M Grid Eleven Composed of Iron Men This Season; Prospects Good For winning Team Despite Small Squad

By Rene A. Henry, W&M Publicity Director
[September 15 – *The Flat Hat*]

Beginning his second season as head football coach, Jackie Freeman will be faced with the problem of fielding a winning team with but 14 returning lettermen and a squad of only 23 men, as compared to 57 last season and 75 in 1951. However, among that handful he will have such outstanding performers as all-American candidate fullback Bill Bowman, end John "Jeep" Bednarik, guard Linwood Cox, who was honorable mention all-America and top choice for all-Southern last season, tackles George Parozzo and "Jarring Jerry" Sazio, a tackle who was inactive last year but whose aggressiveness as a linebacker made him feared by opposing backs during the 1951 season.

This quintet will form the nucleus of the 1953 William & Mary Indians. One thing in favor of the Tribe is the change to the old one-platoon rule, which will serve to offset the lack of depth because of tremendous losses in personnel. With the National Collegiate athletic Association reverting to this limited substitution rule, once more football fans will see the 60-minute man.

Freeman and the coaching staff should be able to field a good starting team, but after the first 15 there is a considerable drop in the caliber of the reserves. Because of this, injuries will very definitely be a determining factor in the fate of the Indians.

The change to the one-platoon rule is highly favored by the entire Big Green coaching staff. The coaches were able to accomplish much in the way of preparing the team for the change during spring drills and worked hard last week to recondition the squad.

With a combined practice (instead of the offensive and defensive units practicing separately) and a small squad, the Indians' coaching staff of Freeman, Eric Tipton, Herb Miller, Johnny Clements, Joe Mark and Sonny Cowling, and freshman coach Boydson Baird were able to spend much more time with each individual player than they had been able to previously.

As a result, all of the squad members had very little trouble I adapting themselves to handling both offensive and defensive assignments. The starting lineup should be well balanced and equally as strong on both offense and defense.

Perhaps the most versatile individual on the team is co-captain Tommy Martin who plays both ways and has handled himself at halfback, guard, tackle and backing up the line. This year he may be used in all, as well as at a starting end berth. At the other end position is another familiar face, John "Jeep" Bednarik. The stalwart Polish tiger has previously been employed as a fullback, center, guard, and last season as an offensive tackle.

Sam Scott has been a starter at an offensive tackle slot the last two years and this Fall will move into the guard slot, and may even see action at center. Holding down the center position is a reconverted guard, co-captain Steve Milkovich. He and Scott may possibly shift on occasion.

Linwood Cox, the 170-pound mighty-mite guard who has held a starting guard position for two seasons may at times see action as an end or center. Sophomore flash Bill Marfizo, who was set to break into the lineup at either an end or center-linebacker position, will be out for an indefinite period with a vertebrae injury in the lumbar region. The 195 pounder looked very promising during early drills but is currently hospitalized. His absence will be sorely missed by the Big Green.

The hardest spot to fill will be that of Ed "Meadows' Mioduszewski, the Tribe's great running quarterback. Freeman will employ both diminutive Al Grieco and Charlie Sumner at the signal calling slot. Bob Elzey, who played a lot of ball at a defensive safety position last year, will back up the former. All three can play halfback, and Grieco and Sumner may alternate at quarterback-halfback in the Big Green backfield.

Because of the shortage of offensive ends and a weak passing combination, which the coaches have been working hard to remedy, the Tribe's defenses will more often see them coming out of a running attack than taking to the air. This can also be attributed to a bulk of good running backs.

Leading the ground assault is "Bullet" Bill Bowman (Birmingham, Alabama), 205 pounds of driving fullback. All all-America candidate this Fall, the speedy Bowman last season averaged 6.1 yards per try, ranked fifth in the Southern Conference in rushing, and ripped off a 67-yard off-tackle sprint against the VMI Keydets.

Sophomore Billy Martin, a sensation in Spring drills, will operate the halfback slot. The Korean veteran, who was ineligible as a transfer student during '52, would have been the ace-in-the-hole who could have broken up William & Mary's fabulous "Lonesome Foursome" backfield.

Walter "Shorty" Herrmann and Jack Place, both Korean veterans and defensive halfbacks last year, will share the other halfback slot. Sophomore Doug "Red-Head" Henley will be the only other reserve back.

The line should be strong as long as it lasts. With three men like Sazio, Parozzo and Bednarik anchoring it, it should be rugged. Tommy Martin, Cox and Scott should not be counted out either. Chet Waksmunski will be heavily counted on for reserve duty. A soph this Fall, "Waxy" has developed more finesse and picked up added weight to go along with his experience. He can play both guard and tackle. Junior John Risjord and soph Bill Nagy will also see reserve duty. Risjord, a track dash man and jumper, is a newcomer flankman. Nagy is still hindered somewhat with a knee ailment.

Iron Indians Saved W&M

by Jennings Culley

As part of the school's Hall of Fame festivities next week, the College of William & Mary will salute the team and the coach that carried W&M football throughout its darkest hour.

This would be the Iron Indians of 1953 and their coach, Jackie Freeman.

The team enjoyed a 5-4-1 season, and Freeman was named Virginia's coach of the year.

Not especially glowing credentials, by normal standards.

But in Tribe football lore, the heroics of the Iron Indians and their coach stand as a testimony to a monumental struggle through adversity.

To fully appreciate the team's success, you have to remember just where W&M football was that autumn.

Before and after World War II, W&M was one of the nation's premier teams. The 1942 Indians – an accepted nickname then – were 9-1-1, beating Oklahoma and losing only to North Carolina Pre-Flight. They were the Southern Conference champions.

In 1946, the prewar stars returned, and the Indians finished second in the league with an 8-1-1 record. Rube McCray had succeeded Carl Voyles as coach by then, and W&M rolled through six winning seasons with two bowl appearances.

But in the summer of 1951, it all came tumbling down.

Scandal rocked the campus. There were allegations of transcript tampering by coaches and other malpractice. McCray resigned.

Later came the charges of stolen examinations and players were expelled.

Marvin Bass tried to calm the waters on season but resigned amid the uncertainty and the faculty calls for de-emphasis of athletics.

In stepped Freeman, a star tailback from the '42 team. He was saddled with limited scholarships, slashed budgets, rock-bottom morale.

The Iron Indians represented his finest touch.

The team started the season with only 23 players, one of whom was kicking specialist Quinby "Hadacol" Hines.

They upset Wake Forest in the Tobacco Bowl here on a Hines field goal and then tied Navy. Wins over N.C. State, Virginia Tech, George Washington and Richmond followed.

They were 5-2-1 heading into November.

"By then we were down to 17 players … We'd lost Charlie Sumner, our quarterback, and others with injuries," Freeman recalled. "We ran out of gas … We lost the last two."

"They had to be a great group of guys to stay together like they did."

The team will be hailed at the W&M Hall of Fame dinner April 13. The night before, players of that era will have a testimonial for Freeman.

"I hate to think of what would have happened to the program without him," said Denys Grant, former player. "It was a difficult time … He was a strong man for the job."

Continued …

"He had only 15-16 scholarships. To hold your own against the big teams was an accomplishment."

With such thin ranks, Freeman scoured the admissions office files looking for students who had played high school football and inviting them out for fall practice.

"We had a kid named John Risjord from Kansas City," Freeman said. "We wrote him and he came back. That first practice, some body cold-cocked him and knocked him stiffer than a board."

"The amazing thing was he stuck it out and played the whole year. He was the best example of how they all felt. They tried and they worked … The spirit was unbelievable."

The team was built around a handful of quality players, three of whom went on to the pros.

In the backfield were Sumner, power runner Bill Bowman, Shorty Herrmann and Al Grieco. The line was anchored by John Bednarik, Jerry Sazio, Aubrey Fitzgerald and George Parozzo.

"We had to play both ways back then," said Fitzgerald, a guard on offense and linebacker on defense. With injuries, we had to patch up a new lineup every week. Jackie did a good job of holding it all together.

His players remember Freeman as a hard coach, but a fair, caring one.

"He treated you with respect and dignity," said Grant. "He actually cared about his players, not just on the field, but in the classroom. He encouraged you to focus on your education. He'd check on your to make sure you were."

In time burdened by two losing seasons and the administrator's continued uncertainly over its football goals, Freeman resigned to enter business.

He never lost his love for football. After 21 years in business and with his children grown, he scratched his itch. In 1979 he joined the Virginia Military Institute staff as an assistant.

"It was a blessing for us to get an assistant with such experience," said Bob Thalman, VMI head coach then. "He was a great help. He was a good coach."

Just what the Iron Indians said four decades ago.

Reprinted with permission of Jennings Culley and the *Richmond Times Dispatch* as published March 3, 1996.

W&M v. Wake Forest
September 19 – City Stadium – Richmond, Virginia

Tribe Opens Years Against Deacons in Tobacco Bowl
Rugged Wake Forest Squad Meets Indians
At Richmond As Gridiron Opens for W&M

By Dick Rowlett
Flat Hat Sports Writer
[September 15 – *The Flat Hat*]

The 1953 edition of the William and Mary gridiron Indians will inaugurate the season this Saturday afternoon in the annual Tobacco Bowl game in Richmond against a very strong Wake Forest eleven. The game is a rematch of the game of two years ago when the Tribe upset the Demon Deacons 7-6 on Quinby Hines' conversion in the first Tobacco game.

Last year the Demon Deacons nipped the W&M squad in a 28-21 thriller. This year the North Carolinas crew looks as powerful as the last time around while the Indians, 24 strong, will in all probability be hard pressed to emulate last season's record. The Wake Forest aggregation compiled a none too gaudy 5-4-1 slate last year, but dropped only one encounter in the old Southern Conference.

This year the outcome of the ball game is not crucial in the sense that it counts in any conference standings. The Wake Forest team now is a member of the new Atlantic Coast Conference while William and Mary remains a member of the Southern Conference.

Heading the invaders' cast will be quarterback Sonny George, who runs, passes and kicks extra points. George heads a veteran backfield that includes Billy Churm, Bruce Hillenbrand and Fullback Smokey Brand. Churm and Hillenbrand each tallied once in last years donnybrook at Cary Field and George scored the winning touchdown and added four straight placements.

Since this backfield ran as a unit last season, it is reasonable to expect a smooth functioning running attack. George will also probably take to the air frequently because he had a great deal of success against the Tribe's defensive secondary, as did many of the Indians' opponent's last year. Sophomores Joe White, Dick Marshall and John Parham have been the most sparkling newcomers in the Deacs practice sessions as of late and any one could win starting berths in Saturday's fracas.

At the end posts the Wake Forest squad is blessed with three top-notch performers in offensive regulars Bob Ondilla and Wes Ledford, and defensive star Ed Stowers. Ondilla was second in pass receptions last year for the Demon Deacons. He lost out to the great Jack Lewis, who W&M fans are sure to remember for his great pass catching show last year, including one grab while lying flat on his back which greased the skids under the Indians. Five sophomores comprise the remnant of the Deacons line.

However, this is not an admission of weakness on the Black and Gold's part. Rather, it shows how surprisingly strong the Deacs are this year. The good veteran line material has been shuttled to the sidelines.

No less than four lettermen, including the widely heralded Bob Bartholomew, will watch the opening kickoff from the bench. Sophomores Donni Garrison and Tom Swatzel at tackles, Earl Shields and Tony Trentini at guards and a fifth second-year man, Joe Dupree at center, are listed as tentative starters.

Coach Tom Rogers of the North Carolina crew has not deviated from the early season path that all football coaches seem to pursue in that he has wielded the crying towel both vigorously and effectively. Nonetheless he expects to have evened the series standings with the Tribe at five games apiece by sun-down Saturday night,.

After Saturday's contest the Indian gridders will still not return to the Reservation for two more weeks. They will travel to Annapolis the following Saturday to test a strong Middie team that is expected to rank among the nations' powerhouses and boasts an all-American guard in Steve Eisenhauer.

Fighting Indian Grid Aggregation Upsets Powerful Wake Forest Deacons, 16-14, As Bowman and Hines Star For Victors

By Dick Rowlett
Flat Hat Sports Writer
[September 22, 1953 – *The Flat Hat*]

A tenacious gang of William and Mary Indians grabbed a third quarter lead and made it stand up in Richmond last Saturday afternoon for a 16-14 decision over the Wake Forest Demon Deacons as a crowd of 17,000 screamed with delight.

It marked the Tribe's second appearance and second victory in the annual Tobacco Bowl game. Two years before the Indians decisioned these same Demon Deacons by a 7-6 count. The final margin of victory in both encounters has been the educated toe of Quinby Hines, the biggest little man in college football.

Last Saturday Quinby added one point after touchdown, and then delivered the "coup de grace" to the invaders from North Carolina with a 17-yard field goal from an angle that would trouble many trigonometry teachers, to say nothing of a place-kicking specialist.

After a beautiful pre-game parade the teams got down to playing football rather abruptly. Charlie Sumner momentarily lost the opening kick-off and could only get back to the 12-yard line. This seemed to be the key for the entire first quarter's play.

The Tribe was bottled up deep in their own territory throughout the whole first stanza and spent most of the quarter fielding the punts off the toe of Sumner. Twice Wake Forest threatened, once they advanced as deep as the five yard line only to have Captain "Sonny" George try a solo, minus blockers, around the W&M left flank. Co-captain Tommy Martin repelled this blast as he did all others.

The Deacons finally got a break when guard Tony Trentini flopped on Sumner's fumble on the Indian 23. Three running plays gained eight yards before John Parham, the Baptist's outstanding performer, raced around right end, found his path blocked, reversed his field and raced around the other end for the longest 15-yard touchdown run of the young season.

After George converted the 7-0 tally loomed large in the minds of Tribe fans who had watched the Big Green sputter on the ground and fail to go in the air-lanes, but they were in for a pleasant surprise.

Sumner, after picking up four yards on his own handed the ball to the Indians' most fared runner, "Bullet Bill" Bowman, and the swift fullback proceeded to gallop 71 yards to a score obtaining two beautiful blocks along the way from "Jeep" Bednarik and Sam Scott. Hines converted and the teams headed for the locker rooms at halftime, tied 7-7.

It took the Indians until the middle of the third quarter to mount another real drive. Bowman and Jack Place led a ground attack that carried to the ten yard line from which came help in the form of Hines' field goal. Now the Tribe was beginning to warm up to the task. They soon had another touchdown just two plays after they regained the ball.

Bowman raced 42 yards on the first play. He was caught from behind by George, who in turn was caught by one of Bill's knees, and although both went down, only Bowman got up. After George was carried off, Sumner uncorked the prettiest run of the afternoon when he raced over the Deacon right guard, jumped and twisted away from a multitude of Wake defenders and raced across the goal line standing up. Hines had already been in so Sumner tried the extra point, but it was blocked.

Churm Tallies

The Deacons returned the compliment immediately by tallying in two plays. Billy Churm took a hand-off and raced 55 yards to the Indian five. Parham carried it over from there. After that it was merely to see if the tiring Tribe could hold off a desperate last gasp Wake drive.

It turned out they could despite the fact that George's substitute, Joe White, booted a punt out of bounds on the one-foot line. George returned to action at the four minute mark, but his efforts were not particularly impressive.

For the outmanned Indians it was a glorious victory. The front wall to a man surprised almost everyone with its tremendous defensive play. George Parozzo, Jerry Sazio, Steve Milkovich, Aubrey Fitzgerald and Lindy Cox all had their moments as did the rest of the line.

However, it was pass defense that the Tribe really excelled in this sweltering afternoon. George spent much of his time eating the ball, thanks to the hard-charging Indian forward wall. And the defensive secondary of Place, Sumner and "Shorty" Herrmann hit the Wake receivers so hard that at the finish they were watching the tacklers more than they were the ball.

Score by Periods
William & Mary 0   7   0   9 -- 16
Wake Forest 0   7   0   7 -- 14

William and Mary scoring: Touchdowns – Bowman (run 71), Sumner (run 33). Conversion – Hines. Field goal – Hines (17).

Wake Forest scoring: Touchdowns Parham 2 (run 15, run 5). Conversions – Frank, George.

The Lineups

William & Mary
Left end – T. Martin.
Left tackles – Sazio, Copeland.
Left guards – Cox, Fitzgerald.

Wake Forest
Left ends – Stowers, Lee, Ledford.
Left tackles – Bartholomew, Frank, Garrison.
Left guards – Huth, Brookshire.

Center – Milkovich.
Right guard – Scott.
Right tackles – Parozzo, Waksmunski.
Right ends – Bednarik, Marfizo.
Quarterbacks – Sumner, Grieco.
Left halfbacks – W. Martin, L.Q. Hines.
Right halfbacks – Herrmann, Place.
Fullbacks – Bowman, Henley

Centers – Soltis, Dupree.
Right guard – Trentini.
Right tackles – Littleton, Swatzel.
Right ends – Ondilla, Whims, Croston.
Quarterbacks – George, White.
Left halfbacks – Parham, Brincefield, Behrman,
Right Halfbacks – Churm, Bland, Frederick.
Fullbacks – Bruce, Hillenbrand, Maravic.

The Statistics

Wake Forest		W&M
10	First Downs	5
252	Rushing Yardage	103
0	Passing Yardage	59
252	Total Yards	162
3-6	Passes Completed-Attempted	4-16
2	Passes Intercepted	1
8-34	Punts-Punting Average	5-39.7
1	Fumbles Lost	1
50	Yards Penalized	10

INDIAN OF THE WEEK

The arrival of King Football back onto the college scene is the time to welcome back another familiar figure along with him – the "Indian of the Week." Every week from now until the football season ends your *Flat Hat* sports staff will vote and decide who the Indian of the Week is for the preceding Saturday's contest.

This week the *Flat Hat* award goes to Fullback "Bullet Bill" Bowman, the Tribe's crunching runner and blocker, who wreaked so much havoc with the favored Demon Deacons. Bill ripped into the Baptists backfield again and again in piling up a tremendous amount of yardage on the ground.

Bill gained 174 yards in 14 tries for an average of 12.4 per carry. He was never thrown for a loss the entire game. He backed up the line with a vengeance and caught the fleet Wake Forest back, Billy Churm, from behind to prevent a sure touchdown.

Bill is a 6'2" 201 pounder who player his prep ball at Riverside Military Academy. He is almost as proficient in the classroom as on the gridiron which is a rare attribute indeed for a football player. Bill is also one of the standbys for Eric Tipton's baseball team, hitting over .300 for the second straight year.

Special honorable mention goes to the beloved little place-kicker, Quinby Hines. Quinby booted a 17 yard field goal as well as adding one extra point to provide the margin of victory. He is, judging by fan applause, the best liked football player in Virginia. However, we feel that without Bowman's running, Quinby would never have been set up in the first place.

The other honorable mention posts fall to George Parozzo and Jerry Sazio, who both did yeoman work on defense. Parozzo called the defensive signals, while Sazio backed up the line and was the man on the bottom of the pile time and time again.

Co-Captains Martin and Milkovich Lead Undermanned Tribe

By Mac McDaniel
Flat Hat Sports Writer
[September 22, 1953 – *The Flat Hat*]

Guiding the touch but under-manned William and Mary eleven this fall are two fighting linemen, Steve Milkovich and Tommy Martin. The co-captains, both seniors, are seasoned veterans in the college pigskin sport and highly capable of their additional leadership duties on the gridiron.

The pair of Indian field generals, in addition to both being to-notch men in the Tribe forward wall, are comparable in several respects. Both Martin and Milkovich display about the same stature. The former player stands 5'11" and checks in at about 205 pounds while the latter carries 195 pounds on similar 5'11" frame.

In football experience the same situation exists. Both of the big Indian linemen have played under the old single wing and now the T-formation. Martin is perhaps the most versatile member of the team. Tommy played tackle last season and may see service this fall at a halfback post as well as his starting end spot. Milkovich, a guard in '52 has been converted to center this year.

Still another way in which the Tribe co-captains parallel is in their academic standing. Martin, a physical education major, is a Dean's List student, while Milkovich, an accounting major, racks up better than average grades and in high school was the recipient of the Danford Foundation Award, given on the basis of athletic and scholarship achievement. Martin, a burly redhead is 24-years old and a native of Roanoke. In high school, "Red Dog," as he is tagged, won all-City, all-County and all-State honors. Later at Camp Lejune, N.C., Tommy played the grid game with Harry Agganis, the "Golden Greek" from Boston University and William and Mary's Jack Place.

Served With Marines

Following his training at Lejune, Martin served with the U.S. Marines in Korea as a 2nd Lieutenant. After his discharge from the Leathernecks the husky redhead returned to the Reservation. Tommy is married and makes his home here in Williamsburg the year round. On campus he is in the Varsity Club and served as pledge master of the Sigma Alpha Epsilon fraternity.

The "Weed," as Milkovich has been nicknamed, hails from Johnston, Penn., and is 22 years old. Steve played a lot of football in the Pennsylvania city and was named to numerous sectional and all-state all-star teams. In his senior year Milkovich was selected on the Class AA team, the highest classification of high school ball in the state.

Steve, in addition to football, is very active in campus activities. He is a member of the Varsity Club, the Accounting Club and treasurer of the Lambda Chi fraternity.

Both of the Tribe co-captains, like everyone else, are well aware of the lack of reserves on the Big Green team. Both players feel that the death of the old two platoon system will prove a lifesaver to Jackie Freeman's eleven. Milkovich commented, "The one platoon system will help up a lot this year with the size of our squad. The going will be tough anyhow, but it would have been much tougher."

In the Martin-Milkovich combination the Indians have a pair of stalwart linemen and highly efficient field leaders. The tribe has undoubtedly chosen two first rate co-captains to lead the team in this big season of uncertainty.

W&M v. Navy
September 26 – Thompson Stadium – Annapolis, Maryland

Tribe Invades Annapolis For Clash With Middies
Strong Middie Team Opens Campaign
Against Underrated Big Green Eleven

By Dave Heinrich
Flat Hat Sports Writer
[September 22, 1953 – *The Flat Hat*]

Fresh from their upset victory over Wake Forest's Demon Deacons, the William and Mary Indians will face a difficult assignment this Saturday against Navy at Annapolis. Coach Freeman's charges looked exceptionally well against the Deacons but against Coach Eddie Erdelatz's Middies they will find one of the most powerful teams the Academy has put together in some time.

Leading the Navy team is a lineman familiar for all those who saw last year's W&M encounter. He is none other than Steve Eisenhauer, who made almost everyone's all-America last year and is an almost sure bet to repeat this year.

Last season Eisenhauer was used exclusively on defense as a middle guard. This year he will play offensive guard under the one platoon rule as well as defensive linebacker. Coach Erdelatz states that Eisenhauer is playing the linebacker position very well which is bad news to all Navy opponents This is the first time he will be used at this position.

Big Tackle

The ends are Jack Rieser and an ex-tackle, Don Fullam, while the tackles are 219 pound Jack Perkins and Hugh Webster. The former was injured for over a week but is expected to be ready for the game.

Eisenhauer's cohort at the other guard position is Jim Leach, while Captain Dick Olson is at the center post. Olson is one of the top centers in the East and should be one of the stalwarts in the Navy line which averages a comparatively light 198 pounds.

The backfield consists of John Weaver, Bob Hepworth, Phil Monahan and Joe Gattuso. Gattuso is the team's only returning linebacker but he is highly regarded by his coaches as an offensive fullback.

The squad of 36 players is made up of 14 lettermen and a host of sophomores up from last year's excellent plebe team. At least seven of these are given an excellent chance to see plenty of action this year. They are ends John Hopkins and Ron Beagle, tackle Pat McCool, guard George Textor and backs Bob Craig and Jim Rundle.

Beat Tribe

Last season the Middies scored 14-0. The touchdowns in this game were scored by Fred Pranco and Fred Brady, both of whom have since graduated.

Commenting several weeks before the start of the season Erdelatz had this to say, "Our new attack will operate with split-T spacing, designed for power between the tackles and geared to throw on every running play. I've been waiting for a good passing quarterback ever since I've been here and now I have two, Weaver and George Welsh., the latter up from the plebes."

The Tribe should be at full strength for this game despite the injuries and bruises suffered in the Wake Forest game. The Indians will have the advantage of having one game under their belt while this will be the opener for the Midshipmen. The Indians will be out to avenge last years set back and should give the Middies a good battle.

Tribe Holds Highly-Favored Middie Eleven To 6-6 Tie At Annapolis As Grieco Sparks Late Offense That Almost Nets Triumph

By Dave Heinrich
Flat Hat Sports Writer
[September 29, 1953 – The Flat Hat]

The William and Mary Iron Indians stunned the football world as well as Navy by battling the Middies to a 6-6 tie before 13,000 fans at Thompson Stadium, Annapolis, last Saturday.

Coach Jackie Freeman's charges weren't rated any better than a two touchdown underdog, but once again they upset the experts and put on a great show of courage and topflight football.

The sparkplug of the Indians squad was diminutive Al Grieco, sophomore reserve quarterback who came off the bench in the second half to lead his team to glory. It was Grieco, with his accurate passing and brilliant running, who took the Navy defense, up to this point, unyielding, by complete surprise.

After the Middies had grabbed a 6-0 lead in the third quarter and threatened to add to their margin, a fumble and a 15 yard penalty set up the tying mark for the Indians early in the final stanza. Navy's star fullback, Joe Gattuso, fumbled on his own 30 where Grieco recovered for the Tribe. An unnecessary roughness penalty against the Middies moved the ball to the 15.

Martin Scores

On third down from the 15, Grieco threw a pass to Tommy Martin who ran into the end zone almost unmolested. Hadacol Hines' attempt for the extra point never materialized as a bad pass from center was fumbled by Grieco. Hines, nevertheless, picked up the ball and tried to run it over but was brought down on the five yard line.

After this touchdown, the Indians had two more opportunities to score but were unsuccessful. Navy punted to the Big Green's 33 from where the Indians moved to the Middies 28 but Martin then fumbled a pass which was recovered by Navy's Bob Hepworth.

A few minutes later, a fumble by Gattuso was recovered by Bill Marfizo on the Navy 47. With Grieco's passes and the running of Shorty Herrmann and Doug Henley, the Tribe moved the ball to the Navy 17 yard line where Hines attempted a field goal. His effort went for naught as a Navy lineman blocked the kick.

Marfizo almost won the game for he Indians a minute later when he rushed in attempting to block a Middie punt near the goal line. He got there a second too late and received a kick in the stomach for his noble efforts.

The Indians had a break in the opening minute of the game when Herrmann recovered a Navy fumble on the Middie 31. The Tribe was unable to move the ball however and the first of many excellent punts by Charlie Sumner went out of bounds on the Navy six.

The Middies moved the ball from here to the Indians' 33 before they were stopped. The balance of the second quarter resembled the first: long, high punts by Sumner continually keeping the Indians out of danger.

The first time Navy got their hands on the ball in the second half they scored. Jack Garrow, who led all ground gainers with 115 yards in nine carries, ran over right tackle for 62 yards and a touchdown. The try for the extra appoint was wide and gave Navy a 6-0 margin.

The Middies came roaring back the next time they had the ball to reach the Tribe five yard line before Herrmann intercepted a pass in the end zone for a touchback.

From the 20 yard line the Tribe moved to the Navy 14 before the drive bogged down at the close of the third quarter.

The game was an inspiring moral victory for the Tribe. Coming on the heels of last week's upset of Wake Forest, many experts are calling the Indians the "miracle team."

Almost every member of the Tribe played well although Bill Bowman was stopped cold by the Navy line. Steve "Ike" Eisenhauer, Navy's all-American, was a big factor in their line although he did not play a spectacular game. But the dominant factor in the contest Saturday was that William and Mary courage and never-say-die attitude which they displayed throughout the afternoon.

Score by Periods
William & Mary 0   0   0   6 -- 6
Navy 0   0   6   0 -- 6

William and Mary scoring: Touchdown – T. Martin (15, pass from Grieco).
Navy scoring: Touchdown – Garrow (62, run)

The Lineups

William & Mary
Left end – T. Martin
Left tackles – Sazio, Copeland.
Left guards – Fitzgerald, Cox.
Centers – Milkovich, Marfizo.
Right guard – Scott.
Right tackle – Parozzo.
Right end – Bednarik.
Quarterbacks – Sumner, Grieco.
Left halfbacks – W. Martin, Hines.
Right halfbacks – Place, Herrmann.
Fullbacks – Bowman, Henley.

Navy
Left ends – Beagle, Navy, Rienier.
Left tackles – Perkins, Kozischeck.
Left guards – Eisenhauer, Textor.
Centers – Olson, Davis/
Right guards – Leach, Arnois.
Right tackles – Webster, Owen.
Right ends – Fullam, Hopkins.
Quarterbacks – Weaver, Welsh.
Left halfbacks – Hepworth, Werness.
Right halfbacks – Monohan, Craig, Garrow.
Fullbacks – Gattuso, Padbeerg.

The Statistics

W&M		Navy
9	First Downs	13
105	Rushing Yardage	241
88	Passing Yardage	83
193	Total Yards	324
12-18	Passes Completed-Attempted	6-17
9-35	Punts-Punting Average	4-33
2	Fumbles	3
25	Yards Penalized	27

INDIAN OF THE WEEK

For the second time in two weeks, the "Indian of the Week" award goes to a back. Unlike last Tuesday, however, it goes to a reserve back. Al Grieco, who wasn't even a starter in the Navy game, richly deserves the designation this time.

The Navy defense was tight during the first half since they knew that Charlie Sumner would not be passing too often and that most of the Tribe's offense would be on the ground. The Navy line held the Indians to 41 yards on the ground during the first half.

When Grieco was put into the game in the second half, he immediately loosened the Navy defenses with his passes. When this was accomplished, the Indian's powerful running game was able to get started and for most of the second half it was William and Mary in control.

It was Grieco who recovered a fumble early in the fourth quart to set up the Tribe's touchdown which he himself had a hand in when he passed for 15 yards to Tommy Martin for the score. Grieco completed 10 of 13 passes for 85 yards and ran nine times for 39 yards to lead the Indians in both departments.

Al is a sophomore from Newark, New Jersey. He is only 5'8" and weighs but 160 pounds. A mathematics major, Grieco is a member of Sigma Nu.

Charlie Sumner, Bill Marfizo, Shorty Herrmann and Aubrey Fitzgerald all receive honorable mentions this week. Sumner's punts and his work at defensive safety were helpful in keeping Navy at bay for the entire first half.

The line play of Marfizo and Fitzgerald was superlative as both of them, sophomore servers, came in time and time again to thwart Navy advances. Herrmann was on the opposite end of several of Grieco's passes besides doing a fine job at defensive halfback.

W&M v. Cincinnati
October 3 – Nippert Stadium – Cincinnati, Ohio

W&M Upset Express Heads West For Bearcat Tilt
Indians Seek To Surprise Strong U.C. Team In Third Straight Away Contest

By David Rubenstein
Flat Hat Sports Writer
[September 29, 1953 – The Flat Hat]

Fresh from their startling tie game with Navy last week, the Indians of the College of William and Mary travel to face the University of Cincinnati Bearcats this Saturday night at Nippert Stadium.

Cincinnati has beaten the University of Tulsa and has lost to Marquette this season. In defeating the Golden Hurricanes 14-7, the Bearcats broke the Oklahoman's 22 game home winning streak. Marquette, a very heavy and fast team, tromped over the Ohioans 31-7 on Saturday night.

This encounter will mark the second time that the Tribe has faced the Midwesterners, having beaten them 20-14 in 1950. According to Assistant Coach Boyd Baird, "Cincinnati is a rough, heavy club which is three deep in most positions."

The men from the Ohio valley have 24 returning lettermen on their squad led by co-captains Don Del Bene and Don Fritz. They also boast one of football's finest head coaches, Sid Gillman. His teams have won the amazing total of 64 games while losing only 16 and tying two for an outstanding .800 winning percentage.

In Gillman's' four year stay at the Ohio school, the Bearcats have always ranked among the top 50 teams in the nation. A thorough technician of just about every phase of the game, Gillman has stressed perfection football. He is recognized as the founder of the two platoon system in most quarters.

Leading the home forces from the quarterback slot will be sophomore Mike Murphy. He is one of the most widely heralded players to come up from the frosh in many years. Murphy has been tabbed as a future Gene Rossi. Rossi was Cincinnati's honorable mention all-American quarterback last year.

The halfback positions will be filled by two veteran running stars. Harry Andreadis and Del Bene. "Hustling Harry" turned in a fine 5.7 yards per try rushing average in his last five games last year. Del Bene is a fine starter and was first in pass receiving with 28 caught for 372 yards.

The Bearcats employ a combination of the spinning and split-T attacks. Their passing game will not be as strong as last season due to the loss of Rossi, one of the nation's top air men. The loss of John Mooth, one of the finest booters in Cincinnati's history will be a severe loss to their punting game.

"Hadacol" Hines is going to be challenged in this game by Ralph Pisanelli. He ranked ninth in the country last year with 29 conversations in 39 attempts. Hines was ranked seventh with 28 PATs with 32 tries.

Fine Ends

Cincinnati has two fine performers at the end posts. Glen Dillhoff and Don Fritz are seasoned veterans of many grid campaigns and should provide good targets for quarterback Murphy. Both boys were popular choices on the all-State team last season and Fritz is definite all-American material in 1953.

Pisanelli at left tackle, Ken Wolf at left guard, Dave Faulkner at the center slot, Bob Marsh at right guard and Noel Guyet at right tackle comprise the middle of the Bearcat forward wall. Each of these men weigh over 192 pounds.

The starting fullback in the Marquette game was Joe Miller, a veteran who was discharged from the service last summer. While a freshman he was a winner of the Frank Hostock award as the outstanding back of the undefeated 1949 team, beating such former stars as Rossi, Glen Sample and Jack Delaney.

A fine runner, strong blocker and good defensive player, Joe should be an outstanding two-way player. Joe Coneilla is also available for duty at fullback. He was first string last year and was the Bearcat's leading ground gainer.

Last year Cincinnati was seventh in the nation in total offense with 38.2 yards average per game. They were also fifth in the country in passing offense with 156 yards per game.

W&M Enjoys Week's Respite After Bearcat Ordeal
Cincinnati Hands Tribe Worst Setback In Many Seasons With 57-7 Rout In Arc-light Contest At Nippert Stadium

By Nate Carb
Flat Hat Sports Editor
[October 6, 1953 – *The Flat Hat*]

Last Saturday night, before a crowd of about 18,000 overjoyed fans at Nippert Stadium, the University of Cincinnati Bearcats hung a 57-7 trouncing on a dogged but under-manned William and Mary football team.

The loss was the worst defeat for an Indian eleven in 39 years. Back in 1923, Syracuse University pasted the Braves 61-3.

Coming on the heels of two magnificent showings against Wake Forest and Navy, the Big Green simply was in no shape for the tussle.

The Bearcats were rough and tough and let the Tribe in on the secret early in the first quarter. Their hard-charging line and speedy backs made a shambles of the game before the first quarter ended with the score 20-0.

With about four minutes gone in the game the Cats, who had previously fumbled on the Indian 21, received a Charlie Sumner kick on their own 20. One play later Dick Goist took a handoff from Mike Murphy and ran down the left end for an 80 yard touchdown.

The Indians received, but when Dave Faulkner soon recovered a Big Green fumble, the Bearcats hit pay dirt again in two plays. On second down, Murphy faked a handoff, then gave to Dick Pardini who circled right end for 31 yards and the score. This time Ralph Pisanelli's conversion was good and the Bearcats led 13-0.

Back came Cincinnati again in less than two minutes. Murphy returned a Sumner punt to his own 38, and on third down passed to Ed Dilhoff on the W&M 49. On the next play Dilhoff snared a long aerial on the 20 and ran over unmolested for their third touchdown. Pisanelli converted again and the home team led 20-0 as the fans went wild.

By this time the Tribe was about to go wild too, but in another way unfortunately. Coach Jackie Freeman had withheld his ace tackles, Jerry Sazio and George Parozzo from the W&M starting lineup because both men were suffering from knee injuries.

However, after the first Cincy score, both boys came in to try and stem the tide. Despite heroic efforts on the part of both, combined with "Jeep" Bednarik, Sam Scott, Lindy Cox and co-captains Steve Milkovich and Tommy Martin, the Big Green line was just not physically up to it.

Cincinnati played a rough tough game and Coach Gillman kept sending in fresh blood. As time wore on the Braves became progressively more tired, and the Bearcats certainly didn't help the situation with their knock-em down, drag-em out brand of ball.

Before the half ended the score had snowballed to 30-0. Fordy Maccioli kicked a 17 yard field goal early in the second quarter and minutes later Goist went over again from the eight. Maccioli's conversion was good and the half ended with the Cats even knocking on the Tribe door again.

Rough Half

Probably it was the worst first half in many, many years for the Gray and Green. Despite a shakeup in the backfield that saw Al Grieco go to quarter, Sumner moved to half and Doug Henley replace Bill Bowman at the fullback slot, Freeman's charges never could mount a serious drive.

At the end of the third quarter the score had snowballed to 43-0. By this time the Braves were in very bad physical shape. Sazio crippled throughout the game and playing under what must have been a terrible physical handicap, finally bowed out to the applause of the fans.

Subs Sizzle

Meanwhile, Gillman's fresh subs ran wild. Joe Miller rocked through center for 18 yards and the score. Pisanelli converted and Cincy led 37-0. Late in the quarter Murphy hit Don Fritz in the end zone and when Maccioli missed the kick, the Bearcats walked off the field 43-0.

Finally the Big Green rolled to its only score early in the last period. With Grieco handling the ball well, they ground to their own 35. There Sumner took the ball on a reverse and went to the Cat 41 and on the next play, Charlie ran over right tackle, broke into the clear, and sprinted 41 yards to pay dirt. Bucky Hines converted.

Ice The Cake

Late in the game Cincy put some icing on the cake with two quick tallies. Joe Concilla intercepted a loose ball on the W&M 39, drove to the two, and then bucked over. Despite a 15 yard clipping penalty, Will Hundemeer still booted the extra point.

With the score 50-7, Erv Single recovered the onsides kick on the Tribe 44. Five plays later Jack Hill broke center and went over for the final tally. This time Irv Turner converted and the final score read 57-7.

Score by Periods
William & Mary .....0 0 0 7 -- 7
Cincinnati.......... 20 10 13 14 -- 57

William and Mary scoring: Touchdown – Sumner (run 43). Conversion – Hines.
Cincinnati scoring: Touchdowns – Goist 2. Pardini. Dillhoff. Miller. Fritz. Concillo. Hill. Field Goal – Maccioli. Conversions – Pisanelli 3. Macciolo. Hundemeer. Turner.

The Lineups

William & Mary
Left ends - T. Martin, Riley.
Left tackles - Copeland, Sazio.
Left guards - Cox, Fitzgerald.
Centers - Milkovich, Marfizo.
Right guards - Scott, Karschner, Nagy.
Right tackles - Parozzo, Waksmunski.
Right ends - Bednarik, Risjord.
Quarterbacks - Sumner, Grieco.
Left halfbacks - Place, B. Martin.
Right halfbacks - Herrmann, Elzey.
Fullbacks - Bowman, Henley, L.Q. Hines.

Cincinnati
Left ends – Del Fino, Schaurrenberger.
Left tackles – Pisanelli, Maccioli, Godkowski, Green.
Left guards – Wolf, Campbell, Knight.
Centers - Faulkner, Single.
Right guards – Marich, McCain.
Right tackles - Buyet, Snyder, Walsh, Jenike, Ritchey.
Right ends – Dillhoff, Maudeon, Nenis.
Quarterbacks – Murphy, Necisek, Hundemer.
Left halfbacks – Pardini, Turner.
Right halfbacks – Goist, Del Fino, Hill.
Fullbacks – Concilla, Conaster.

The Statistics

W&M		Cincinnati
7	First Downs	25
124	Rushing Yards	347
7	Passing Yards	209
131	Total Yards	556
1-11	Passes Completed-Attempted	9-13
1	Passes Intercepted	2
8-35	Punts-Average	2-31.5
3	Fumbles Lost	2
6	Yards Penalized	60

INDIAN OF THE WEEK

In a game which produced few individual stars, at least on William and Mary, Charlie Sumner certainly rates as the outstanding local player in the 57-7 Cincinnati defeat last Saturday and thereby earns the nod as *Flat Hat* "Indian of the Week."

Charlie started off the game at quarterback, but he had very little luck at this slot, and was moved to left halfback early in the game when Al Grieco came in to call the signals. Pretty much stymied in the first half, Sumner nevertheless managed to get off a couple of fine punts.

However, it was in the third and fourth periods that the junior from Salem came into his own. He wound up the game with 86 yards gained in eight tries, including two spectacular runs of 24 and 41 yards, respectively.

Both of these sprints came in the last quarter, were consecutive, and resulted in the Big Green's only touchdown of the evening. Sumner punted six times for 218 yards and a 36 yard average, and generally was the best Indian player out there on the field, as everybody who saw the game agreed.

Honorable mention this week goes to a number of William & Mary players who stuck in there despite painful injuries. Leading the array is tackle Jerry Sazio, who could hardly walk when the game ended. George Parozzo, "Jeep" Bednarik, Bill Marfizo, Tommy Martin, Lindy Cox and Steve Milkovich all played their hearts out in a losing cause. Finally, Al Grieco, who spent most of the evening trying to pass in the face of a pack of Bearcat linemen who rushed him, must rate a nod of approval.

W&M v. Virginia Tech
October 17 – Cary Field – Williamsburg, Virginia

Indians Open Home Season With Game Against VPI
Powerful Gobblers Bring Dean's Arm Plus 3-1 Record Into Cary Field Clash

By Mac McDaniel
Flat Hat Sports Writer
[October 13, 1953 – *The Flat Hat*]

With probably the toughest portion of the 1953 grid schedule behind them and after a week's layoff from the football wars, the William and Mary Indians open their home campaign at Cary Field Saturday with Virginia Tech.

The Gobblers from Blacksburg are undoubtedly the top team in the Old Dominion this Fall, displaying a current 3-1 log which includes victories over Marshall, the University of Virginia and the University of Richmond.

Coach Frank Moseley's Orange and Maroon eleven opened the season with an unimpressive 7-0 win over Marshall, but then surprised U.Va. at Charlottesville by a 20-6 count. The next week the Gobblers Northern invasion proved a stumbling block as Rutgers upset the visitors 20-13. However, last Saturday Tech resumed its winning ways topping Richmond 21-7.

The Gobblers will need the Indians' scalp this week end if they expect to remain at the top of the Big Six. The air arm of Johnny Dean combined with the terrific Tech ground game will undoubtedly pose a tough problem for Coach Jack Freeman's eleven.

The VPI clash will mark the 28th meeting of the two schools. In the previous contests both institutions have won 12 games while a trio of contests has ended in stalemates. Last season at Blacksburg, the Tribe punished the Gobblers 35-15.

Tech, with 27 returning lettermen, lost only three seniors from the 1952 squad. Coach Moseley, who took over the reins as head mentor at VPI in 1951, may realize one of his big gridiron aims this Fall with a championship Big Six eleven. Last year Tech came out on the short end of a 5-6 won and lost record, but basically the same varsity line-up with a year's additional experience makes the club dangerous this season.

Top Backfield

The Gobblers backfield, particularly on the ground, is one of the tops in the state in this campaign. Spearheading the attack for the visitors will be Jack Williams and Dean, who alternate at the quarterback post. The latter player was given quite a pre-season build-up but he has yet to live up to his highly touted reputation. Williams, a senior, has handled the bulwark of the signal calling.

In addition the VPI backfield boasts Doug Creger, Julian King, Howard Wright, Bill Anderson and Dickie Beard. Beard, a 5'9" soph, handles most of the visitors' extra point booting. Don Welsh and Don Booth move from the tailback spot, with Welsh getting most of the activity. The 6'1" 200-pounder hits the line like a bull and last season averaged over four yards per carry.

Fine Line

The Tech line, averaging about 192 pounds, has given up an average of eight points per contest, or a total of only 33 points in a quartet of games to date.

At the end posts, the Gobblers have a couple of fine performers in Billy Allen and Bob Luttrell, both good pass receivers and defensive stalwarts. Other ends include Charles Herb, Tom Petty, Roger Simmons and John Moody.

Tim Hughes, George Preas, Frank Brown and Tom Richards all see service at the tackles for Tech.

Guard Slot

At the guards are Ernie Wolfe, Harold Grizzard, Jimmy Haren and Bill Kerfott. Rotating at the center slot are Hunter Swink and James Randall. The former girder is attempting to fill the shoes of the graduated Madison Nutter and is doing a great job, particularly as a linebacker.

After a badly needed and heartily welcomed week end off, the Big Green team will have to "turn on the steam" in order to improve the current 1-1-1 record before the home folks Saturday.

Big Green Silences Squawking Gobblers In Thriller
Sumner And Bowman Inspire Gridders To 13-7 Triumph Over VPI Before Capacity House In First Home Fracas

By Mac McDaniel
Flat Hat Sports Writer
[October 20, 1953 – *The Flat Hat*]

With Charlie Sumner and Bill Bowman sparking a powerful offensive attack, the William & Mary Indians toppled the Virginia Tech Gobblers 13-7 before a capacity crowed of 12,500 fans in a Cary Field grid battle last Saturday afternoon.

The decisive W&M victory, under an 80 degree sun, shattered VPI's hopes for the 1953 Big Six championship and set-up Coach Jackie Freeman's "courageous 24" as the top challengers for the Old Dominion football title.

The Tribe offense began to click after the opening minutes of the second period and midway through the quarter W&M hit pay dirt. Sumner returned a Hokie punt from his own 28 to the 43.

Then with Doug Henley and Sumner getting most of the work, the Indians moved steadily on the ground to the VPI eight yard stripe. Bowman replaced Henley at the tailback post and went over for the score on two running plays. Tommy Martin converted to make the count read 7-0, W&M.

Throughout the remainder of the quarter the two teams traded the pigskin back and forth and at the half the Tribe had a first down on the Gobblers' 17.

The final Tribe touchdown came with only 42 second remaining in the third quarter. Following a 40-yard field goal attempt by Tech's Johnny Dean, the Big Green eleven marched from their own 20 to the VPI goal.

Sumner's running and passes sparked the attack as he set up the scoring play on the visitors' one yard marker, handing off to Bowman, who went over right guard for the TD. L.Q. Hines' trusty toe misfired as the placement was wide.

In the fourth and final period the ruggedness and wear and tear of 60 minutes of gridiron competition began to show on Freeman's "Iron Men." After brilliantly repelling a VPI goal-line onslaught, the Indians were finally scored on in the final four minutes of the game.

Recovering a "Bullet Bill" Bowman fumble on the W&M 38, Tech quarterback Jack Williams set-up the score with a pass to end Tom Petty on the four and then went over himself on a quarterback sneak two plays later. Dickie Beard booted the extra point for the Gobblers.

Throughout the course of the afternoon, just as in the Wake Forest and Navy Games, the Tribe line played outstanding ball. Chet Waksmunski and Humphrey Copeland made very commendable showing at the tackles, replacing injured line stalwarts Jerry Sazio and George Parozzo. Jeep Bednarik and Bill Marfizo also played a fine line game.

Great Defense

Particularly spectacular Tribe defensive play was exhibited early in the final period when the Hokies had a first down on the W&M four yard line and were stopped dead on four consecutive rushing plays.

Sumner and Bowman shared the individual honors in the Indian attack. The Salem boy notched 61 yards rushing in eight carries and completed eight of 13 passes for 112 yards, while the "Emporia Express" reeled off 74 yards in 16 trips with the pigskin, a number of which were for first downs.

Pace Team

VPI fullbacks Don Welsh and Don Booth and signal caller Jack Williams paced the Gobblers as the tailbacks were consistent ground gainers while Williams sparked the feeble Tech air arm. The highly touted Johnny Dean was almost a total flop, failing to make any ground afoot and unable to complete a single forward pass.

The game, the first of the season on the Reservation, was marked by numerous injuries. Only two penalties were called, both against the Indians. The Tribe lost six yards when interference was called on Bob Elzey on a second period pass play, and five yards in the final minutes for too much time in the huddle.

The W&M victory was the 12th straight time the Tribe has beaten VPI, as the Gobblers are still looking for their initial win in Williamsburg. The triumph was the second of the campaign for William and Mary, as Freeman's gridders now show a 2-1-1 record.

Score By Periods
Virginia Tech 0   0   0   7 -- 7
William & Mary . . . 0   7   6   0 - 13

VPI scoring: Touchdown – Williams (run 3). Conversion – Beard.
William and Mary scoring: Touchdowns – Bowman 2 (run 3, run 1). Conversion – T. Martin.

The Lineups

Virginia Tech
Left ends – Simmons, Herb, Petty.
Left tackles – Hughes, Richards.
Left guards – Kerfoot, Haren, Burleson.
Centers – Wink, Randall.
Right guards – Grizzard. Wolfe.
Right tackles – Press, Brown.

William & Mary
Left ends – T. Martin, Riley
Left tackles – Copeland, Waksmunski.
Left guards – Cox, Karschner.
Center – Marfizo.
Right guards – Milkovich, Fizgerald.
Right tackle – Scott.

Right ends – Moody, Lutrell
Quarterbacks – Dean, Williams.
Left halfbacks – Creger. Burke.
Right halfbacks – Beard, King, Anderson, Scruggs.
Fullbacks – Welsh Booth.

Right end – Bednarik.
Quarterbacks – Sumner, Grieco.
Left halfbacks – W. Martin, Elzey, Hines.
Right halfback – Herrmann.
Fullbacks – Bowman, Henley.

The Statistics

VPI		W&M
11	First Downs	20
146	Rushing Yardage	210
35	Passing Yardage	112
181	Total Yardage	322
2-9	Passes Completed-Attempted	9-15
1	Passes Intercepted	1
5-46	Punts-Average	5-37
1	Fumbles lost	3
0	Yards penalized	11

INDIAN OF THE WEEK

On whom are we going to bestow the honor of "Indian of the Week"? After every W&M pigskin battle this is the question confronting the *Flat Hat* Sports Staff. Last week the solution was simple after "Bicarbonate"* modestly produced the photo of shapely Mamie Van Doren and himself.

Editor's Note – A nickname for Flat Hat Sports Editor Nate Carb

This week for the second consecutive time, we feel that we can hand out the orchids without too much deliberation as Charlie Sumner is undoubtedly the man for the award.

The 6'1" quarterback from Salem, in notching the Indian of the Week honor for the second time this season, was instrumental in the Tribe's 13-7 win over VPI. The 195 pound signal caller completed eight of 13 passes, picked up 61 yards in eight carries, had a 38-yard punting average and a 61.6 yard kickoff average.

Bill Bowman, 200 pound fullback, who scored both Indian TD's and chalked up 74 yards on the turf, heads the list on honorable mentions. Others deserving of honorable mention include Bob Elzey, Jeep Bednarik and Chet Waksmunski.

W&M v. George Washington
October 24 – Cary Field – Williamsburg, Virginia

Colonials Provide Homecoming Rivalry As Indians Seek Second Straight Victory Against Conference Clubs This Saturday

By Dick Rowlett
Flat Hat Sports Writer
[October 20, 1953 – *The Flat Hat*]

An invading bunch of Colonials from George Washington University are preparing to spoil the Homecoming celebration of students and old grads alike this Saturday when they storm onto the Reservation to do battle with Coach Jackie Freeman's fighting Tribe eleven.

The Indians have established themselves as the best in the Southern Conference this side of the mountains, which means that West Virginia has been discounted for a moment. The Big Green will be giving everything they have in an effort to add luster to their national reputation for being "Iron Men."

The Colonials will carry a 2-2 record into the game. They opened impressively by beating VMI 14-13 on two conversions by Dick Gasperi and the next week they measured North Carolina St. 20-7 on the pitching arm of quarterback Ray Fox. Fox, one of the conference's best aerial artists, has found himself delegated to the second string now that two-platoon football has made it demise.

The past two weeks have been frustrating ones for Coach Ron Sherman. First Virginia beat a touchdown path to the GW door for a 24-20 victory and then last week the West Virginia powerhouse administered a 27-6 defeat in a Friday night game in Griffith Stadium.

Anchoring an all-letterman line for the visitors will be Captain Steve Korcheck, a big 200 pound center that everybody is booming for all-Conference. Steve is a senior, as are five of the probable starters, and is also a 60-minute man doubling as a line backer on defense.

The guard slots are manned by rugged Carl Bodelous, a 215-pound senior "rock" from Pottstown, Pennsylvania and next to Korcheck, probably the ranking defensive player on the team, and Dick Gasperi, the place-kicking specialist who stands at seven out of nine for the season.

Three seniors head the tackle corps for the Blue and Yellow. John Prath at 212 pounds and Tom Bosman at 190 hold forth on the left side of the Colonial line. Dick Drake, a 204 pounder is the right tackle incumbent.

At end the Colonials are even tougher. In left end Richie Gaskell they have the ranking pass catcher in the Southern Conference. This 195 pounder snagged two pay-off pitches against Virginia and is big and rough. The other flank position is patrolled by last season's defensive starters Pat Kober and George Dunen.

In the all important quarterback slot the Colonials have not one but two outstanding performers in Ray Fox and Bob Sturm. The latest statistics from Conference headquarters show that GW is leading in pass offense. Sturm, last year's safety man, ranks number one right now because he is a great asset defensively.

At the beginning of the year observers thought that the Colonials would do well on the ground but have little power in the airlanes. Such has not been the case since Coach Sherman has developed a down-right lethal air offense to go with his good ground game.

At halfbacks the invaders will uncork a multitude of hard-running backs led by the terrific Len Giemniecki, a 210 pounder who has been among the Conference's best for three years. Bill Wever will probably draw the starting nod at the other halfback position. Saffer, Dick Phillips, Arlin Barr and Lou Donofrio will all see action as the afternoon progresses.

The fullbacking duties are handled by he veteran Dutch Danz, a power runner galore from the old school. Danz is "Mr. Inside" to Ciemeniecki's "Mr. Outside." Joe Boland, a hustling 190 pounder is a player who would be first string on many other squads around the state. The Colonials' season this year has so far been marked by sparkling offensive play coupled with a defense that tends to be inconsistent.

Tribe Stymies Colonials' Last Minute Bid As Sumner's Goal Line Pass Interception Provides Thrills For Homecoming Crowd

By Dick Rowlett
Flat Hat Sports Writer
[October 27, 1953 – *The Flat Hat*]

A never-say-die bunch of William and Mary Indians held for four downs on their own nine yard line in the last minute and a half to beat an underrated George Washington team 12-7 last Saturday before 7,000 deliriously happy fans.

From the William and Mary nine yard line, with 1:31 remaining on the scoreboard clock, the Colonials had a first down, goal to go. First Dutch Danz, the games' leading ground gainer, and then Bob Sturm hit the middle for a yard.

From the seven Sturm was stopped for no gain. On fourth down Sturm pitched o Ted Saffer, who fired a pass into the end zone. However, the ball never arrived as Charlie Sumner, who had been fooled earlier on the same play, intercepted and the ball game drew to a close.

Strange Contest

It was a strange contest in that the Tribe had only two chances to score and capitalized on both, while GW must have set a new record for ground gained between the 20 yard lines.

After stopping a GW drive on their own 22 late in the second period, the Big Green took off on a scoring jaunt in nine plays. Al Grieco fired a pitch-out pass to Shorty Herrmann on the W&M 34. Then Sumner fired a 32-yarder to Bill Bowman on the Colonials 34.

It was the good right arm of Sumner once again as he fired to Bowman for a first down at the seven yard line. From there Bowman went two, Sumner went three, and Herrmann crashed over right tackle for the score. One minute and thirty seconds remained on the big clock as Steve Korcheck blocked Quinby Hines' extra point attempt.

Knock At Door

The second half had hardly begun when the Colonials were once again knocking on the door to touchdown territory. From their own 38 they advanced to the Big Green's 15 yard line and where Sturm missed connections on two scoring passes. The Colonials finally got their break when Korcheck intercepted Grieco's pass on the William & Mary 33.

Sturm lost no time in firing one to Richie Gaskell, who made a tremendous one hand scoop of the ball at the 12 yard line. Two plays later Sturm raced to the one yard line and he scored on the next play. Dick Gasperi booted the extra point and the homestanding team trailed 7-6.

The situation brightened quickly when Bowman ran a twisting kickoff back 37 yards to the GW 33, almost going all the way. Sumner and Bowman managed to pick up a first down to the 21 as the quarter ended.

On third down from the four yard line Sumner broke over right guard for the score and then missed the placement with 13 minutes remaining.

Score by Periods

George Washington 0   0   7   0 -- 7
William & Mary 0   6   0   6 -- 12

George Washington scoring: Touchdown – Sturm (run 1). Conversion – Gasperi.
William and Mary scoring: Touchdowns – Herrmann (run 3). Sumner (run 4).

The Lineups

George Washington
Left ends – Gaskell, Daly.
Left tackles – Drake, Bosmans.
Left guards – Neal, Gasperi.
Centers – Korcheck, Nedran.
Right guards – Bodolus, Solomon.
Right tackle – Ziamandonis.
Right ends – Kober, Darcu.
Quarterbacks – Sturm, Fox.
Left halfbacks – Ciemniecki, Saffer, Phillips.
Right halfbacks – Weaver, Barr.
Fullbacks – Danz, Boland.

William & Mary
Left end – T. Martin
Left tackles – Waksmunski, Copeland.
Left guards – Cox, Fitzgerald.
Center – Marfizo.
Right guard – Milkovich.
Right tackles – Scott, Parozzo.
Right ends – Bednarik, Risjord.
Quarterback – Sumner.
Left halfbacks – Elzey, Grieco, Hines.
Right halfback – Herrmann.
Fullbacks – Bowman, Henley.

The Statistics

George Washington		W&M
21	First Downs	9
263	Rushing Yardage	119
115	Passing Yardage	97
378	Total Yardage	216
10-20	Passes Completed-Attempted	6-10
1	Passes Intercepted	1
3-36.3	Punts-Average	3-36
0	Fumbles Lost	0
35	Yards Penalized	25

INDIAN OF THE WEEK

For the first time this week a lineman is the recipient of the "Indian of the Week" award. George Parozzo entered the game early after Chet Waksmunski was shaken up and proceeded to play 50 odd minutes of outstanding football. Parozzo was a demon on defense and contributed several key tackles.

Special honorable mention goes to Sam Scott, Waksmunski, and Jeep Bednarik. These three boys were at the bottom of the pile again and again. Scott also flashed some fine blocking on offense to set up the winning score.

Also honored this week are backfield aces Bill Bowman and Charlie Sumner. Bowman was the Tribe's leading ground gainer per usual and played well defensively, while Sumner's passing was the Indians main weapon and he also ran well when the occasion demanded.

W&M v. North Carolina State
October 31 – Riddick Stadium – Raleigh, N.C.

Big Green Iron Men Tackle N. C. State At Raleigh
Five Consecutive Defeats To Indians Plus Highly Rated Passing Offense Spark Wolfpack In Seeking Revenge

By Mac McDaniel
Flat Hat Sports Writer
[October 27, 1953 – The Flat Hat]

After the humiliating 41-6 shellacking at the hands of Jackie Freeman's Indians on the Reservation last season, the North Carolina State Wolfpack will undoubtedly be "up" for Saturday's grid battle in Raleigh.

Although State under the reins of Horace Hendrickson hasn't gone anywhere in particular this Fall, the home eleven will naturally be seeking sweet revenge. The Wolfpack to date claims only one winning decision, a 27-7 conquest of Davidson.

In four other contests, leaky Sate defense and a slow moving attack have spelled defeat. The quartet of setbacks, however, have been administered by some of the top teams in the South. Hendrickson's club fell before the University of North Carolina 29-7, then stumbled 29-7 before George Washington, followed by the Davidson triumph.

Wake Forest's Deacons hit the Wolfpack 20-7 the next week and then last Saturday State was thumped solidly 31-0 by Duke,

If the boys from Raleigh are to improve on last season's poor 3-7 record, they will have to hit the victory trail very shortly. After five consecutive losses in the past five campaigns to William and Mary, and after the way things have gone this year, State would like nothing better than to upend the Tribe this Saturday,.

Despite State's miserable record in games played this Fall, the team has done much better statistically-wise than would be expected. Red and White ranks sixth in rushing offense, but third in aerial offense, in the Atlantic Coast Conference. Not including the figures from the Duke contest, the Wolfpack also ranks third in the conference in total defense having given up 210 yards per game.

Coach Hendrickson has a big squad but boasts only 17 returning lettermen. Operating out of the T-formation, the Wolfpack's backfield includes Eddie West and Carl Wyles at quarterback, Colbert Micklem, Chris Frauenhofer, Dick Bethune and Bill Teer at the halfbacks and Don Langston and Joe Barringer at the tailback post.

West and Wyles spearhead the State passing attack and rotate calling signals. Langston, running from the fullback slot, is the Wolfpack's candidate for all-American. The six foot 200 pound junior chalked up 488 yards on the ground in 100 carries with the pigskin last season, and although not as effective this Fall, he still poses quite a threat offensively.

At ends for N. C. State are Henry Brown and Dave Gebhard. Also available are Harry Lodge and John Thompson. Wolfpack tackles include Bob Paroli, Ken Urgovitch, C.M. Price and Anthony Leone, a converted guard.

The center of the forward wall is composed of Ed Mazgaj, Charlie Davis, J.W. Frankos, Al D'Angelo, Jim Frazier and Jim Bagonis at the guard posts and Dick Tonn and Ralph Mueller at center.

Freeman's Iron Indians Defeat State As Line Checks Late Wolfpack Drive

By Nate Carb
Flat Hat Sports Editor
[November 3, 1953 – The Flat Hat]

A William and Mary line which had played heads up ball all afternoon, held in the final two minutes last Saturday to give the Big Green a thrilling 7-6 victory over N.C. State in Raleigh. Earlier in the fourth period, Aubrey Fitzgerald, the Indians' right guard, had broken through to block Al D'Angelo's try for the extra point and insure the margin of victory.

Nevertheless, the victors' cause looked black indeed when, with less than five minutes left in the game, reserve quarterback Al Grieco fired a pass from his own 20 and Bill Teer, Wolfpack halfback, intercepted and ran to the W&M nine.

With a formerly hushed State Homecoming crowd on its feet, the Braves braced for their second goal-line stand of the contest. Paul Smith tried the middle for one. On the next play he took a pitchout and cut wide to the left. Bob Elzey and Jeep Bednarik stormed through, chased Smith back to the 15 where Elzey dumped him in his tracks, and virtually killed the rally then and there.

With third down, Sate quarterback Eddie West flipped a pass to Don Langston in the end zone, but Elzey leaped high and broke it up. Desperate, D'Angelo was sent in to try a field goal, but West elected to use him as a decoy, and fired a pass to Smith on the 10, which was dropped.

Bowman Fumbles

The Big Green took over on downs and ran out the remaining two minutes, but the game still wasn't in the bag for fullback Bill Bowman promptly fumbled on the 16, and the ball squirted back to the 10, where Quarterback Charlie Sumner desperately dived on it. Sumner then ate up the clock with plunges over the line, and the Tribe held on to win.

After a scoreless first half, where both teams threw away golden chances to score, William and Mary game to life in the third quarter, receiving the opening kickoff and marching 70 yards for the score.

Grieco brought the kick back to the 30, where three plays later, Sumner handed off to Bowman, who knifed to the 49. On second down, Grieco took a handoff and raced over right tackle to the 41. Then Bowman ripped to the 32 and Shorty Herrmann bulled for the first down to the 28.

With the Green and Gray rolling on the ground, the State line braced and caused Grieco to fumble. The ball rolled to the 14, where Bednarik alertly fell on it before a host of 'Pack gridders lunged in vain.

Bowman then bulled eight and on third down, took a handoff from Sumner and streaked around right end for the tally. Little Quinby Hines then came in and booted the try for the extra point, providing the Tribe with what was later to prove the margin of victory.

Fumbles Hurt

William and Mary threatened to bust the game wide open later in the quarter but time and time again they were stalled, usually due to fumbles. Twice they got deep into State territory, once on a fine pass from Sumner to Elzey, and again on an interception by Herrmann, but on both occasions, Bowman fumbled first on the 32, then on the seven.

With the opportunity staring them in the face, the Wolfpack finally came to life in the last period. West, who played well all afternoon, shot a 47 yard pass to Teer, who raced to the Tribe 27 before Doug Henley brought him down. On second down, fullback Langston bolted to the 15.

Smith then took a handoff from West, circled to the left and romped over, untouched. Here D'Angelo came in, but before he could even get set to try the conversion, Fitzgerald stormed through and blocked his kick completely.

State nearly scored in the second quarter when Grieco fumbled a punt and Teer recovered on the Tribe 21. Running plays over the center of the line, the losers advanced to the four, but on third down, an end-around play failed and they finally were stopped just short of a first down a foot from the W&M one.

Score by Periods
William & Mary ..... 0 0 7 0 -- 7
North Carolina State ... 0 0 0 6 -- 6

William and Mary scoring: Touchdown – Bowman (run 8). Conversion – Hines.
North Carolina State scoring: Touchdown – Smith (run 7)

The Lineups

William & Mary
Left ends - Risjord, Riley.
Left tackles - Copeland, Cox.
Left guards – Waksmunski.
Centers - Milkovich, Marfizo, Karschner.
Right guards - Scott, Copeland.
Right tackles – Parozzo.
Right ends – Bednarik.
Quarterbacks - Sumner, Grieco.
Left Halfbacks - Hermann, B. Martin.
Right Halfbacks - Elzey, L.Q. Hines.
Fullbacks – Bowman.

N.C. State
Left end – Lodge.
Left tackles – Urgovitch, Price.
Left guards – Mezgaj, Kass.
Centers – Tenn, Mueller, Vivanna.
Right guards – D'Angelo, Frazier.
Right tackles – Dunnagin, O'Bryant, Urgovitch.
Right ends – Brown, Reed.
Quarterbacks – West, Wyles.
Left halfbacks – Teer, Kilyle.
Right halfbacks – Micklam, Smith, Mendlock.
Fullbacks – Langston, Nordona.

The Statistics

W&M		N.C. State
17	First downs	9
182	Rushing Yardage	110
56	Passing Yardage	64
6-13	Passes Completed-Attempted	4-15
2	Passes Intercepted	2
4-35.3	Punts-Average	5-33.2
4	Fumbles Lost	1
45	Yards Penalized	55

INDIAN OF THE WEEK

Jeep Bednarik, who has been playing a fine game of football at right and for William and Mary all year, burst into spectacular prominence last Saturday as he led his mates to a 7-6 victory over N.C. State. For this he earned the *Flat Hat* award as "Indian of the Week."

It was Jeep who recovered a fumble by teammate Al Grieco on the State 14 to set up the Tribe's lone score. Later in the game he broke through the Wolfpack forward wall and chased Paul Smith back to the W&M 15 where Bob Elzey nailed him, probably saving the game for the Big Green then and there.

Earlier in the second quarter, Bednarik charged into the 'Pack backfield and literally stole the ball from Carl Wyles, making the State quarterback look very foolish indeed. Playing virtually the entire game, the senior from Bethlehem, Penn., was a granite pillar on defense all day, and also caught two passes for big gains when the Tribe was attacking.

Honorable mention goes to Bill Marfizo and Chet Waksmunski, who backed up the line very effective, Steve Milkovich, a 60 minute man at center, and backs Charlie Sumner and Shorty Herrmann, who both played consistent ball.

W&M v. VMI
November 7 – Victory Stadium – Roanoke, Virginia

Big Green Flies To Roanoke For VMI Charity Clash
W&M Seeks Fourth Consecutive Win
Against Keydets Led By Shifty Mapp

By Dave Rubenstein
Flat Hat Sports Writer
[November 3, 1953 – *The Flat Hat*]

The "Iron Indians of 1953" riding on the crest of a three game winning streak, travel to Roanoke this Saturday to face a hard luck team from Virginia Military Institute in a benefit Shrine game.

Leading the upset minded Keydets into this fray will be their talented halfback and co-captain, Johnny Mapp. At the moment he is the leading ground gainer in the State and second in total offense in the Southern Conference, a sure bet for all-Conference and all-State honors.

VMI will be out to avenge a 34-13 setback at the hands of last year's Indian aggregation, administered in the same Victory Stadium in last season's opener for both clubs. They will also seek to break a two game losing streak in this, their eighth encounter of the campaign,

Coach John McKenna's squad showed that they could run up a score when they downed Catawba 44-0 in this year's inaugural. George Washington spoiled the Homecoming festivities of the Keydets by taking a hard fought contest, 14-13, the following Saturday,

The taste of defeat was destined to remain with the Soldiers one more week as they bowed to the Spiders of Richmond, 13-7, in their third test of the season. The men from Lexington won their next two in a row, defeating the Citadel and Virginia, 14-0 and 21-6 respectively.

West Virginia, the nation's fifth ranked team, was just too much for the Keydets to handle on Saturday afternoon. They succumbed by the lopsided score of 52-20. Last week Coach McKenna's crew was upset by Florida State, 12-7.

Along with their experienced scat back, Mapp, VMI boasts 20 returning lettermen and a squad of 41 players. They are four deep in every position except fullback. Dave Woolwine, the first string quarterback, works out of the T-formation.

At the end posts, Coach McKenna has two experienced men, Charlie Byrd and Bill Ralph. Both are big, over 215 pounds each, and very fast. George Ramer, the Keydets' other co-captain, starts at the tackle slot along with Buck Boxley. Ramer is considered the best lineman on the squad.

Playing the guard positions are Joe Siler and John Morgan. Rounding out the starting line at center is Karl Kliner, a first stringer at Lexington for the third season. Dave Woolwine is given support at quarterback by junior Royce Jones and sophomores Jimmy Foster and Dick Fencel.

Not enough mention can be given to Mapp. He is VMI's pride and joy; a first string A.P. all-Southern halfback.

VMI Touchdown In Last 57 Seconds Upsets Indians 20-19 In Shrine Game

By Mac McDaniel
Flat Hat Sports Writer
[November 10, 1953 – *The Flat Hat*]

Halfback Johnny Mapp leaped high into the air to snap Dave Woolwine's 23 yard forward pass in the end zone in the final seconds of play to give the VMI Keydets a tight 20-19 win over William & Mary's "Iron Indians" in the third annual Shrine classic at Roanoke last Saturday afternoon.

The game, played before 5,000 frost-bitten fans under a clear November sky was almost a duplication of the 1950 meeting between the two schools when VMI shoved across a last minute score to take a 20-19 decision over the Big Green.

Although the Tribe escaped without any serious injuries, the loss, only the second of the campaign, was certainly a three-fold defeat for W&M. The upset wrecked the Tribe's bid for the Big Six Crown, the Southern Conference Championship, and a post-season bowl bid.

Quick Score

The Indians scored the first time they got their hands on the ball when Charlie Sumner went over from the one yard stripe, capping a quick 76 yard march midway in the first quarter. Although Tommy Martin's placement attempt was wide, it looked as though the Tribe had things well in hand.

However, only minutes later, the whole outlook changed, as the Lexington eleven recovered a Sumner fumble on the W&M 25. At the end of the period VMI had a first down on the Big Green four yard line.

A stubborn goal line stand with key tackles by Doug Henley, Bill Marfizo, Jeep Bednarik and Sumner gave the Indians the pigskin inches away from their own end zone.

This moral victory was short-lived however, as several plays later the Red, White and Yellow capitalized on a 15-yard Tribe penalty for illegal use of the hands, and galloped for a TD. Mapp carried the mail into pay dirt from the nine and Woolwine converted.

Before the end of the half Coach John McKenna's boys again made good use of a break as they turned a Sumner pass interception into a second tally. Following two rapid first downs, Woolwine plunged over for the Keydets and then booted the extra point with 40 seconds of play remaining in the period.

The Tribe opened the second half with a bang, scoring on three plays after the kickoff. Martin returned the punt from his own 23 to the 49 and then Bill Bowman broke loose and thundered down to the Keydet one yard line before being knocked out of bounds. Sumner scored through the middle on the keep and Martin converted to bring the Indians within one point of VMI.

Midway in the same third period W&M again began to march. With Bob Elzey, Sumner and Bowman lunging the leather, the Big Green added another six pointer. It was

"Bullet Bill" who climaxed the scoring drive with an 11 yard line sweep. This time Martin's conversion was no good, but the Tribe held a five point 19-14 margin.

After vaulting into the lead, Freeman's "Iron Men" began to show the effects of the hard fought battle, and VMI soon started to threaten. Unable to move on the ground, the Keydets began to shower the sky with aerials.

With time running out and a first down on the W&M 23, Woolwine connected with an accurate pass into the arms of the speedy 165 pound Mapp for the tally. Lindy Cox deflected Woolwine's extra point boot, but the one point 20-19 lead proved to be sufficient.

The Tribe came roaring back and managed to grab two quick first downs and were on the Keydets 39 with a first and ten when the clock ran out, as the Keydets notched a mild upset.

Score by Periods
Virginia Military Institute . . . 0 14 0 6 -- 20
William & Mary 6   0 13 0 -- 19

VMI Scoring: Touchdowns – Mapp 2 (run 5, pass from Woolwine 23). Woolwine (run 1). Conversions – Woolwine 2.
W&M Scoring: Touchdowns – Sumner 2 (run 1, run 1). Bowman (run 12). Conversion – T. Martin.

The Lineups

VMI
Left ends – Byrd, Doodley.
Left tackles – Miller, Westfall.
Left guards – Morgan, Lazarus.
Centers – Klinar, Poss.
Right guard – Boxley.
Right tackle – Ramer.
Right end – Ralph.
Quarterback – Woolwine.
Left halfback – Lavery.
Right halfback – Mapp.
Fullback – Servidio.

William & Mary
Left end – T. Martin.
Left tackles – Waksmunski, Sazio.
Left guards – Cox, Fitzgerald.
Center – Marfizo.
Right guards – Scott, Copeland.
Right tackle – Parozzo.
Right ends – Bednarik, Risjord.
Quarterback – Sumner.
Left halfbacks – Elzey, Grieco.
Right halfback – Herrmann.
Fullbacks – Bowman, Henley.

The Statistics

VMI		W&M
13	First Downs	16
151	Rushing Yardage	248
135	Passing Yardage	51
286	Total Yardage	299
8-13	Passes Completed-Attempted	3-10
2	Passes Intercepted	0
4-33.8	Punts-Average	5-34
1	Fumbles Lost	1
15	Yards Penalized	34

INDIAN OF THE WEEK

For the second time this season "Indian of the Week" honors go to the Tribe's hard-running fullback, "Bullet Bill" Bowman. The "Emporia Express" has ranked high among the leading ground gainers in the Southern Conference all season, but in Saturday's contest with VMI at Roanoke the big fullback really broke loose.

Bowman carried the pigskin on 15 occasions for a total of 127 yards and was on the receiving end of three passes against the Keydets. "Bullet" pushed his total offense yardage for the campaign to 504 and owns a 6.5 yard per carry average, tops in the Old Dominion.

In addition to his offensive feats in the Roanoke clash, Bowman also played a terrific game on defense. Usually employed as a flanker, Bowman made numerous tackles in the secondary.

Charlie Sumner, six foot quarterback, heads the list of honorable mentions. Other Indians earning mention include a trio of linemen, Bill Marfizo, Chet Waksmunski and Georg Parozzo who were all in on numerous tackles.

W&M v. Richmond
November 14 – City Stadium – Richmond, Virginia

Big Green Journeys To Richmond To Oppose Spiders
Merrick's Surprising Gridmen Battle W&M In Important Big Six Contest

By Doug Rowlett
Flat Hat Sports Writer
[November 10, 1953 – The Flat Hat]

One of the biggest "grudge" battles in years is the prospect for this Saturday when the Big Green grid machine, looking for revenge after last Saturday's heartbreaker, invades Richmond for the big traditional clash with the Spiders of Richmond.

Both teams have lost one game in Big Six play and therefore the winner will become the top contender for the all-Virginia crown. Richmond has wins over Randolph-Macon 27-0, Davidson 13-0, VMI 13-7, Washington & Lee 27-20 and Boston College 14-0. Their only setback came at the hands of VPI 21-7, and they also played a 13-13 tie with Wake Forest.

Three years of recruiting has finally paid dividends and Coach Ed Merrick's Spiders seem to have escaped the "habitual tailenders" tag hung on them in past years. Saturday's contest at City Stadium is being played up by the Richmond press as the game of the year in Virginia.

A homecoming crowd of around 20,000 fans is expected to jam in to the stadium to watch one of Virginia football's bitterest rivalries. These two teams have met 62 times and the Richmond crew holds a two game edge, 29-27, with six ties. Last year at Cary Field the Indians sank the capital city crew 41-14.

Genial Les Hooker, Richmond cage coach, has scouted the Tribe for the past two weeks, being seen by reliable sources in both Raleigh and Roanoke. Les also scouted the Big Green last year when the Spiders suffered a 41-14 shellacking at the hands of Ed Mioduszewski and Company.

Leading the Spider eleven from the all important quarterback slot are Ted Theodose and Bill Bauder. These two alternate throughout the game and one of them has been hot every game this season. Theodose is the better runner of the two and leads the Spiders in total offense, while Bauder holds the passing edge.

Hold Back Slots

The halfback positions in this two platoon system fall to Ed Elliott, Lewis Wacker and Roland Evans at left half and Ralph Scarpo and Don Arey at right half. Elliott is the best of this lot. Besides being a good runner, he is an excellent pass catcher and a tremendous defensive halfback.

The fullback post is capably handled by Frank Pajackowski and "Corky" Jones. Both of these 185 pounders can move well on the ground and are good blockers. Johns has been hampered by injuries for the third straight year.

The end posts on this year's Richmond team fall to Eric Christensen, who was all-State selection as an offensive tackle two years ago and Maurice Thacker, a 205 pound rock on defense.. Les Androcronis, Jim Brier, Phil Carley and Paul Sheridan, all lettermen, lend support for the flank position.

Five veteran tackles, led by big Walt Garcia and Red Keville, four lettermen guards, paced by placekicker Bobby Sigro, and two veteran centers in Al Pecuch and John Gavlick give the Spiders a tremendous defensive line.

Sparkling Line Play Helps Iron Indians Take Easy Victory At Richmond 21-0

By Dave Heinrich
Flat Hat Sports Writer
[November 17, 1953 – The Flat Hat]

The Richmond Spiders, who have been weaving a web to catch the Iron Indians all season, evidentially got entangled in it themselves as they fumbled five times to lose 21-0.

Before the game was give minutes old, the Tribe had themselves a touchdown and were on their way to a second when an intercepted pass halted the drive and prevented what well may have been an unexpected rout.

In the third quarter, a 60-yard drive netted the Indians' second touchdown and a pass interception by Bob Elzey in the waning moments of the game set up the final score with only 17 seconds left.

The Spiders fumbled on the first play from scrimmage on their own 47 and Bill Marfizo recovered. With Billy Martin finally running as his advanced notices had stated, the Indians moved to the 20 yard line where Bill Bowman, in two thrusts through the line went over for the score.

For the first time this year Jerry Sazio was called on to kick the extra point and Jarring Jerry put the ball through the uprights for a 7-0 lead.

More Fumbling

It seemed that the Spiders, if they had any desire to win, waned to do it the hard way because they fumbled the next time they got the ball and it seemed as if the Indians were on their way again as Billy Martin carried to the 16. But a Sumner pass was intercepted by the tight Richmond pass defense, and the threat went by the boards.

A Richmond drive late in the first period was started by a recovered fumble and ended when Richmond's' Ralph Scarpo fumbled on the Tribe three. This was the closest Richmond came to scoring all afternoon.

The second quarter was not too spectacular although two plays of particular note did take place. After the Indians had been forced to punt deep in their own territory, Chet Waksmunski came charging up field and literally stole he ball out of Bill Thacker's hands.

This was easily the outstanding defensive play in the game, although the play of Waksmunski on defense all afternoon was a thing to behold.

The other play was a runback of a punt by Ed Elliott towards the end of the first half. He went down the sidelines for 39 yards before Bill Marfizo pushed him out of bounds.

Long Drive

A long Indian drive in the middle of the third quarter set up the second Indian score. A 10-yard run by Herrmann and a 12 yard Sumner-to-Elzey pass brought the ball to the Richmond six.

Bowman then electrified the crowd with a leap over the entire Spider forward wall for a first own on the three. Two more thrusts at the line by the Emporia Express produced the market.

Hines Converts

Since it was the waning moments of the quarter when Bowman went over, Quinby Hines came off the bench and booted his first of two extra points.

Early in the fourth quarter, the Big Green recovered a fumble deep in Richmond territory but the drive stalled on the two yard line. The Spiders tried frantically to get some sort of desperation drive started throughout the fourth quarter but the rugged Indian line, obviously well-coached by Neepie Miller, could not be budged.

Miller, by the way, was taken sick on Monday morning and rushed to the local hospital where his illness was diagnosed as appendicitis. However, he is getting along fine and is expected to recover quickly.

After Elzey had intercepted a pass late in the fourth quarter the Indians moved to the four where a Spider offsides penalty brought it to the one. After two plays, Al Grieco, who had replaced Sumner at quarterback, sneaked over. Hines again converted to make the final score read 21-0.

Personal Record

The Tribe set some sort of personal record by employing 22 players. There were no injuries other than the usual assortment of cuts and bruises, although co-captain Steve Milkovich sat out the entire game with a leg injury,

Outstanding in the Tribe offense were Herrmann, Billy Martin and Bowman. The lineman all played well with Waksmunski, Sazio, Marfizo and George Parozzo leading the way.

Throughout the afternoon it was apparent that the Spiders were stopping Sumner on the option play but they were unable to stop Bowman or the hard running Tribe halfbacks and that told the story.

Score by Periods
```
William & Mary  ......  7  0  7  7 -- 21
Richmond ............  0  0  0  0 --  0
```
William and Mary scoring: Touchdowns – Bowman 2 (run 5, run 1). Grieco (run 16). Conversions – Sazio. Hines 2.

The Lineups

William & Mary
Left ends – T. Martin, Riley.
Left tackle – Sazio.
Left guards – Waksmunski, Nagy.
Center – Marfizo.
Right guards – Scott, Copeland.
Right tackles – Parozzo. Karschner.
Right ends – Bednarik, Cox, Risjord.
Quarterbacks – Sumner, Grieco.
Left halfbacks – W. Martin, Hines
Right halfbacks – Herrmann, Elzey.
Fullbacks – Bowman, Henley.

Richmond
Left ends – M. Thacker, Curley.
Left tackles – Keville, Liebich.
Left guard – Sgro.
Center – Pecuch.
Right guards – Hallinan, Berry, Witt.
Right tackles – W. Thacker, Frostick, Garcia
Right ends – Christensen, Brier.
Quarterbacks – Theodose, Bauder.
Left halfbacks – Elliott, Wacker.
Right halfbacks – Arey, Scarpo.
Fullbacks – Pajaczkowski, Johns, Gavlick.

The Statistics

W&M		Richmond
12	First Downs	8
186	Rushing Yardage	121
41	Passing Yardage	6
227	Total Yardage	127
5-10	Passes Completed-Attempted	1-8
1	Passes Intercepted	2
6-21.1	Punts-Average	4-37.7
1	Fumbles Lost	5
37	Yards Penalized	45

INDIAN OF THE WEEK

This week's "Indian of the Week" award goes to Chet Waksmunski for his terrific line play against the University of Richmond. Waxy was in on almost every tackle throughout the game. It seemed as if he was all over the field. One play he would be making a tackle o the left side of the line an the next play he would be on the right side.

His outstanding defensive play was when he raced down under a punt and stole the ball from a startled Ed Thacker. Waksmunski's offensive play showed improvement as he threw several key blocks, one of which set up Billy Martin's 19-yard run which led to the Indians' first score.

The 18-year old Waksmunski is the youngest member of the team. He is six feet tall and weights 195 pounds. A sophomore member of Sigma Nu, he is a mathematics major.

Honorable mentions go to Billy Martin for his fine play both offensively and defensively, Bill Bowman, for his usual fine game, and Jerry Sazio, who returned to the wars with a blaze of glory and scored his first collegiate point with a touchdown conversion.

W&M v. Washington & Lee
November 21, 1953 – Cary Field – Williamsburg, Virginia

Big Green Engages Generals After Scalping Spiders
Aroused Washington & Lee Gridmen
Collide With Braves In Big Six Finale

By Dennis Smith
Flat Hat Sports Writer
[November 17, 1953 – The Flat Hat]

This week Coach Jackie Freeman's Iron Indians tackle an aroused Washington & Lee squad in a Big Six battle at Cry Field. The Indians and the Generals are both riding high as the result of last week's encounters. W&L, which has won only three games out of nine, owned the University of Virginia Saturday by a 27-13 count.

The Generals' attack is ably directed by their 165-pound quarterback, Joe Lindsey. Lindsey is playing his last game next week and will undoubtedly be a thorn in the Indians' side. The senior from Galax scored one touchdown against the Cavaliers, while passing for 159 yards and running 50.

The boys from Lexington had played very unimpressive football up until their tilt with Virginia Saturday. The Generals won their opening against Shepherd College and then proceeded to drop the next six to Maryland, North Carolina West Virginia, Richmond, Virginia Tech and George Washington respectively.

Washington & Lee cannot be sold short, however, because they are definitely an improving club. With wins over Davidson and UVa. In their last two outings and with steadily improving line play they will be tough.

Conrad Flanders, a 6'1" 175-pounder from Massachusetts, will probably stat at left half against William and Mary. At the other half will be Eddie Landis, a hard-running touchdown maker from Maryland.

Facing the Tribe at fullback will be Cire Barcellona, who is also playing his last collegiate game. Rounding out the backfield for the Generals is the 60-minute man, Lindsey.

Washington & Lee will field a veteran line which averages close to 200 pounds. Bill McHenry, last year's captain, is holding down the center spot for the third year in a row. McHenry stands 6'3" tall and weights 210 pounds.

At the guard slots are Tom Fieldson and Don Wever. Weaver is playing his firs year as a guard but has plenty of experience due to linebacking chores assigned to him last year.

Bob Lafferty and Harold Brooks will be at the tackles of the Generals. Brooks is the largest man on the squad at 230 pounds. He is also doing the plackicking this season. Harold Sturgill will probably start at right end. Roger Hagey will hold down the other side of the line.

This game is a must for the Tribe if they intend to capture the Big Six crown for which they are still in contention. Even if they beat W&L, however, they will not cop the title unless VMI and VPI tie on Thanksgiving. Otherwise, Virginia Tech will take the laurels.

Invading Generals Blast Big Green 33-7
In Penalty-Ridden Cary Field Encounter

By Dick Rowlett
Flat Hat Sports Writer
[November 24, 1953 – The Flat Hat]

Even a brief appearance in the lineup by ace quarterback Charlie Sumner failed to save the William and Mary Indians from a 33-7 shellacking at the hands of the Generals of Washington & Lee before a sparse crowd of 3,300 people at Cary Field last Saturday. It was the invaders third straight victory in the month of November.

The boys from Lexington turned the game into a rout in the space of eight minutes in the third quarter. Carl Bolt whose name is a personification of his play provided the straw that broke the Big Green's back when he took the kickoff following the Tribe's lone score up the West sideline 92 yards for a touchdown.

The rest of the first half was spent with neither team going anywhere but backward. The defensive play in this frame became particularly aggressive, which is a nice way of saying our boys got tired of being penalized for W&L throwing punches.

The advent of the second half saw Sumner at quarterback. It was evident that he couldn't run on his bad ankle, but even this failed to prevent him from throwing often and effectively. Sumner eventually kicked dead on the invaders' four yard line.

Lindsey's return punt went out of bounds on the Indian 19 and from this spot Sumner fired first a 23 yard pass and then a 27 yard scoring toss to Shorty Herrmann. Herrmann made beautiful receptions on both occasions, spinning right out of at the grasp of two tacklers on his latter grab.

After Quinby Hines had added the conversion, Bolt made his aforementioned jaunt. Sam Scott, the last man with a chance to catch him, was erased by a beautiful downfield block by Ciro Barcellona.

The Big Green stormed back but Sumner had his pass stolen by End Harold Sturgill and from the W&L 46 as the Generals needed just 16 plays to make it 19-7 with Bolt slithering over from the four yard line on second down.

The Lexington aggregation was back in touchdown territory just four plays later when Herrmann's punt from the William and Mary 25 was blocked by tackle Jay Heckmann and picked up by the same culprit for the score.

The next time that the Tribe got possession Al Grieco fumbled on second down and the Blue and While recovered at the Big Green 36. Flanders raced 32 yards around left end to the three yard line where Lindy Cox caught him from behind. It took Bolt two tries to tally this time and Lindsey once again converted.

With the score 33-7 against them the Indians started to roll downfield and twice threatened to score. Once they reached he three yard line before one of the illustrious men in white clouded the issue with an illegal procedure foul.

Injuries to the top two quarterbacks seriously handicapped the Tribe. Sumner complete four out of five passes and showed tremendous courage in the face of a painful injury.

The visitors' line, led by such standouts as captain Bill McHenry and tackles Heckman and Bill Lafferty, until he was hurt, stopped the Indians impressively on the ground and the absence of a passing arm definitely hurt the home team's chances. Halfbacks Bolt and Flanders combined with Bowman to keep the referees from completely stealing the spotlight

Bill Marfizo, who has played fine ball for the Tribe all year, re-injured a vertebrae in his back during he second half and had to be helped off the field.

Score by Periods
Washington & Lee . . . . 0 7 6 20 -- 33
William & Mary . . . . 0 0 7 0 -- 7

W&L Scoring: Touchdowns – Bolt 3 (kickoff return 92, run 4, run 1). Flanders (run 1). Heckmann (blocked punt and run 10). Conversions – Lafferty. Lindsey 2.
William and Mary Scoring: Touchdown – Herrmann (pass from Sumner 27). Conversion – Hines.

The Lineups

Washington & Lee
Left ends – Hare, Buchanan, Dunker.
Left tackles – Lafferty, Manning, Brooks.
Left guards – Fieldson, Baker.
Center – McHenry.
Right guards – Weaver, Dalligatti.
Right tackles – Heckmann, Murphy.
Right ends – Sturgill, Groeneveld, Gillespie.
Quarterback – Lindsey.
Left halfbacks – Bolt, Sargent, Moody.
Right halfbacks – Benham, Flanders, Landis.
Fullbacks – Barcellona, Degree.

William & Mary
Left ends – T. Martin, Riley.
Left tackles – Sazio, Karschner.
Left guards – Waksmunski, Cox, Fitzgerald.
Centers – Marfizo, Milkovich.
Right guards – Scott, Copeland.
Right tackle – Parozzo.
Right ends – Bednarik, Risjord.
Quarterbacks – Elzey, Grieco, Sumner.
Left halfbacks – W. Martin, Henley.
Right halfbacks – Herrmann, Hines.
Fullback – Bowman.

The Statistics

W&L		W&M
16	First Downs	12
254	Rushing Yards	156
32	Passing Yards	85
286	Total Yards	241
3-9	Passes Attempted-Completed	6-17
0	Passes Intercepted	1
5-40	Punts-Average	6-27.8
0	Fumbles Lost	2
100	Yards Penalized	75

INDIAN OF THE WEEK

Walter "Shorty" Herrmann richly deserves the *Flat Hat* "Indian of the Week" award as he was one of the few bright lights in an otherwise dismal afternoon last Saturday. Besides scoring the only Big Green touchdown early in the third period, Herrmann also deserves recognition as a steady ground gainer.

His pass interception in the third quarter temporarily halted the rampaging Generals, as he aptly demonstrated his defensive skill. The 24 year old Herrmann stands 5'10" and tips he scales at 170 pounds. The Warwick halfback is a member of Kappa Sigma social fraternity.

Honorable mentions are awarded to Charlie Sumner for his exceptional punting and all-around play despite a painful ankle, Chet Waksmunski for his usual outstanding line work, and dependable "Bullet Bill" Bowman, the leading W&M ground gainer, who ran 88 yards despite ineffective blocking support.

W&M v. Boston University
November 28 – Cary Field – Williamsburg, Virginia

Terriers Invade Reservation For Last Game of Year
Indians Hope to Snap Back Saturday
Against Highly Rated BU Aggregation

By Dave Rubenstein
Flat Hat Sports Writer
[November 24, 1953 – *The Flat Hat*]

After absorbing an unexpected shellacking at the hands of Washington & Lee last week, the Big Green will undoubtedly be out for revenge against the Terriers of Boston University this Saturday in the last clash of the season for both squads.

Despite the loss of the fabled Harry "Greek" Agganis, the Beantowners will bring a fine team with them. Boston, under the veteran coaching of Aldo "Buff" Donnelli, has had a mediocre season to date, winning only four games against three losses and a tie.

Impressive Wins

The Terriers have defeated Brandeis, Lehigh, Villanova and Temple by very impressive scores. They were trounced by Penn State and Holy Cross, but only lost to Marquette by one point, 7-6,. This decision is very significant because Cincinnati lost to this same Marquette team by over 20 points. Syracuse provided the opposition for the tie game which resulted in a 14-14 stalemate.

William and Mary has faced the New Englanders four times since the series was inaugurated in 1947. The count is now even with each squad having taken a pair. Last year the Indians lost a close one in the last few minutes, 33-28, after having come from behind to go ahead by one point, 28-27. Agganis was the spoiler as he threw the winning touchdown pass.

Most Depth

Boston will have the most depth that the Tribe has seen this year. They are loaded with 43 men, including 25 returning lettermen, and are five deep in every position but center.

If the Braves are to stop the Scarlet and White, they will have to bottle up their diminutive quarterback, John Nunziato. This senior from Somerville, Mass., is only 5"5" tall and weighs but 148 pounds; certainly not very much for a college grid star.

However, "Nunzie" is a very competent signal caller and a great competitor. Also at the position of quarterback is Tom Gastall, the boy who caught the pass from Agganis that beat W&M last year. He is an excellent passer and should keep the Indian secondary on its toes when he is in the lineup.

Another Terrier who will make life miserable for the Braves is halfback Don DeFeudis. Along with his side-kick at the other halfback slot, Bill Taylor, he will provide a stern test for the Big Green forward wall. DeFreudis led the Beantowners in scoring with nine touchdowns last year.

Rounding out the backfield are fullbacks Sam Pino and Mario Moriello. Pino is returning to the Terrier lineup after spending two years in the Marine Corps. He was their top ground gainer in 1950.

Veteran Line

Coach Donnelli has virtually an all veteran line returning to duty on the gridiron. Outstanding on the end posts are bull-like Jim Meredith, ace New England defensive end last year, and little Marco "Scooter" Landon. Landon recovered 14 fumbles of he entire Boston total of 26 which tied Nevada for the nation's lead in that department.

Five lettermen are available for the tackle position and only one of the five weighs under 205 pounds. Captain Ray Cataloni along with Mike Mavropoulos will give the Bostonians plenty of defensive strength at the guard posts. The position of center will be capably handled by John Pappas, a good candidate for sectional honors.

Colonial Echo 1954
(The Flat Hat did not publish the week of Thanksgiving so there is no post-game recap or "Indian of the Week")

Boston University 41; William and Mary 14
[Colonial Echo 1954]

A band of battle-worn Indians took the field against Boston University for the season's finale. Deep in reserve power, Coach Buff Donnelli utilized all his resources for the Tribe defeat. The charging Boston line and explosive backfield left the Big Green trailing by 14 points at the halftime.

The only two deep penetrations by the Indians resulted in touchdowns. With Grieco carrying 18 yards on the option keep play, the Tribe broke into the scoring column in the fourth quarter. Later in the period, Sumner passed to Bowman who eluded the Terrier safeties and ran 25 yards for the second touchdown. Tommy Martin converted the first tally and Hines booted the extra point after the second score.

Outstanding players for the Iron Indians received credit from sports writers over the nation. Bill Bowman reaped in the laurels ranging from honorable mention all-American with Jeep Bednarik to Captain of the all-Big Six team in Virginia, including all-Southern Conference. Sumner, Bednarik and Parozzo were also elected to the all-Big Six team as well as receiving Southern Conference honors.

Score by Periods
Boston University . . . . 14 0 20   7 - 41
William & Mary . . . . 0 0   0 14 - 14

Boston U. scoring: Touchdowns – Terrasi 2, Petroka, Defeudis, Landon, Hagerstrom. Conversions – Terrasi 4, Gastall.
William & Mary scoring: Touchdowns – Bowman (pass from Sumner 34), Grieco (run 18). Conversions – T. Martin, Hines.

The Lineups

Boston University
Left ends – Meredith, Bredicer, Terentino, Salomond.
Left tackles – Mairui, Fraser, Brecker.
Left guards – Cataloni, Johnson, Assad.
Centers – Giuliano, Abbruzzesse.
Right guards – Marvropolus, McNally, Biernacki.
Right tackles – Vendetti, Pednault, Bates.
Right ends – Landon, Pollack, Sobiek.
Quarterbacks – Nunziata, Gastall.
Left halfbacks – Terrasi, Sylvia, Luciano.
Right halfbacks – Defeudis, Chadwick, Hagerstom.
Fullbacks – Petroka, Pino, Soullane.

William & Mary
Left ends – T. Martin, Fitzgerald, Riley
Left tackle – Sazio.
Left guards – Waksmunski, Nagy.
Centers – Milkovich, Marfizo.
Right guards – Scott, Cox.
Right tackles – Parozzo, Copeland.
Right ends – Bednarik, Risjord.
Quarterbacks – Elzey, Grieco, Sumner
Left halfbacks – W. Martin, Karschner.
Right halfbacks – Herrmann, Hines.
Fullbacks – Bowman, Henley.

The Statistics

Boston University		W&M
16	First Downs	11
260	Rushing Yardage	128
132	Passing Yardage	136
392	Total Yardage	264
4-10	Passes Completed-Attempted	9-17
2	Passes Intercepted	2
3-25	Punts-Average	5-26.4
2	Fumbles Lost	3
65	Yards Penalized	5

The Flat Hat did not publish the week of Thanksgiving so there is no "Indian of the Week."

Other Books by Rene A. Henry

Communicating In A Crisis – A guide for management, Gollywobbler Productions, 2008

Offsides! Fred Wyant's Provocative Look Inside the National Football League, Gollywobbler Productions and Xlibris, 2001

You'd Better Have A Hose If You Want To Put Out the Fire – the complete guide to crisis and risk communications, Gollywobbler Productions, 2001

Bears Handbook – Stories, Stats and Stuff About Baylor University Football, co-author with Mike Bishop, Midwest Sports Publishing, 1996

Marketing Public Relations – the HOWs that make it work!, Iowa State University Press, hardcover 1995; ISU/Blackwell/John Wiley & Sons, paperback 2000

MIUS and You – The Developer Looks At A New Utility Concept, co-author with Joseph G. Honick, Fernando Oxaca and Richard O'Neill, U.S. Department of Housing & Urban Development, 1980

How To Profitably Buy & Sell Land, John Wiley & Sons, 1977